FINDING TURTLE FARM

FINDING TURTLE FARM

My Twenty-Acre Adventure in Community-Supported Agriculture

ANGELA TEDESCO

University of Minnesota Press

MINNEAPOLIS • LONDON

Published by the University of Minnesota Press
111 Third Avenue South, Suite 290
Minneapolis, MN 55401-2520
http://www.upress.umn.edu

ISBN 978-1-5179-1161-4 (pb)

Library of Congress record available at
https://lccn.loc.gov/2021062861.

Printed in the United States of America on acid-free paper

The University of Minnesota is an equal-opportunity educator
and employer.

30 29 28 27 26 25 24 23 22   10 9 8 7 6 5 4 3 2 1

For John, Amy, and Kristin,
the loves of my life

CONTENTS

INTRODUCTION

The Seeds of My CSA Adventure

IN JUNE 1999, I stood in a patch of strawberries on the twenty-acre farm my husband and I had purchased the previous year. The unmistakable, fruity fragrance of the ripe berries wafted up in a slight breeze under the hot, summer sun. I could have closed my eyes and, just from the fragrance, known where I was on this piece of ground I was starting to shepherd as an organic farm. I reached down to sample a beautiful berry, bit into its soft, red flesh, and savored the actual fruit of my labor. These berries took the longest of all my crops to grow—they were planted in the spring of the previous year—building intense anticipation of this favorite crop. You cannot find this experience in a grocery store where the berries may have been shipped from thousands of miles away by an unknown farmer or corporation. They may be enticingly big and beautiful, but the amazing fragrance, peak flavor, and soft texture are missing. As I pulled aside green leaves to pluck another berry sitting atop the straw mulch, my thoughts were of how pleasing it would be to share this experience with others. Sharing one's joy can make all the hard work involved in its production worth it. I got that reward every time I packed and delivered the fruits and vegetables from this fertile ground to my CSA members who had signed up to get a box every week for a twenty-week season. This week, those red jewels in their quart containers would be sitting on top of those boxes like flashing beacons.

What did you eat today for breakfast? Lunch? Dinner? Do you know who grew it and how it was grown? Do you know how it got to your table and how long it took? Does it matter to you that the soil that grows plants for your diet is alive and teeming with life—insects, bacteria, earthworms—that transforms nutrients into your food? Does it matter to you if your eggs come from a chicken that can move about in its natural environment, eating its natural diet that can include insects and grasses rather than living its life in a cage being treated like a machine?

It matters to me. And that's why I started a small farm to grow food for people who were also concerned about our food system. Here was a farm that they could visit, a farmer they could get to know and trust and to whom they could ask their questions about how the soil was being treated, how their food was being grown, and then what to do with that wide variety of fruits and vegetables that landed on their plates—a truly local connection. Field days at the farm encouraged visitors to observe or participate in harvesting some crops. Education is a large part of the CSA concept and encourages members to journey through the season with the farmer, identify their vegetables, and learn how to prepare them in the kitchen. Education is also important for the wider community, and whenever possible, I took the time to share information there also. I had to laugh one time when I asked a new restaurant owner if he "bought local," and he replied in the affirmative, "just down the street at the local grocery store."

This book is about my personal journey of bringing food

to the table: from land purchase to soil preparation, from sowing and harvesting to giving my customers a memorable experience. It's also about the journey of that CSA community of people who were willing to put their money where their mouths were, knowing that if one does not support this type of agriculture, it will disappear. Where we put our food dollars matters. CSA customers would pay up front for the season of food to help the farmer finance the work ahead of production regardless of the bounty or bust that lay in their future. They weren't looking for cheap or convenient food necessarily—just healthy food grown in healthy soil. They knew they could eat those strawberries right out of the box without concerns that the fruit held pesticide residues. Fred Kirschenmann, an organic farmer and philosopher, in a speech at a farming conference in 2004 titled "Farmers, Who Needs Them," related, "A staffer from the White House's Office of Management and Budget said if two or three farmers could produce all the nation's food that was fine. In fact, if robots can, who cares?" Contrary to that thought, my customers cared deeply, and they wanted to take this adventure with me.

This book is also about the transformation of a piece of land and the life within it. Removal of herbicide and pesticide use can greatly benefit a piece of ground. These benefits were sometimes obvious, with the return of earthworms and a wide diversity of insects, and sometimes not so obvious, as with the increasing amounts of organic matter and microscopic life in the soil, all part of an entire, balanced ecosystem. And while the fruits of farming are very visible and tangible, I also tried to communicate to my customers, and now you, my readers, the sacred and spiritual side of farming in this interactive dance we do with Nature. I was honored to share this invisible portion of the farming experience with my customers; hopefully, they absorbed some of that along with their box of vegetables.

My early life laid the groundwork for this venture. The fertile soils of Oklahoma's Grady County welcomed me with horned toads and box turtles, tadpoles in lingering spring puddles, crops of cotton and wheat, alfalfa and corn, cattle, always a large vegetable garden, and Lady, our horse. Our dog Fido was the guardian, following my brothers and me everywhere we went on the farm. In this rural setting nine miles from the nearest small town, with no television or nearby neighbor children, my days were spent outdoors whenever possible, forging a connection with Nature that felt natural and necessary. I knew where the water moccasins lived and to stay away from them. I knew not to get between a mother cow and her newborn calf. I knew I had to complete my job of collecting eggs scattered among the stacked hay bales in the barn no matter how much I procrastinated, even if a possum or a snake, those egg-eating connoisseurs, might be there to greet me. Our two-story wooden frame home, complete with lightning rods on the roof, was flanked by a large barn with a hay mow. East of the barn was a small stream, a catalpa tree, a gypsum rock outcropping on the crest of a hill, and a buffalo wallow just beyond. These permanent features of the landscape were visible to the eye, but the spot where Lady was later struck and killed by lightening left no lasting marks except in our hearts and minds.

My father loved farming. Why else would he whistle, literally, as he worked, riding the tractor for endless hours in the field? Hearing that sound from a distance over the drone of the tractor engine was comforting beyond just confirming his whereabouts. But my father gave up full-time farming, which accompanied his full-time job working in Oklahoma City sixty miles away, when he had a minor heart attack. We moved closer to his work but still had the large vegetable garden, some cows, sometimes pigs, dogs that never compared to Fido, and a pond with fish, but not the crops that overextended our father. The red, sandy soils were not as good in Lincoln County, but my father could amend our garden to get good results.

I never planned on becoming a farmer. And when I unexpectedly did, I was certainly not the best suited physically or with mechanical skills. I was born fourth of five children between two brothers. My sisters, who were the oldest, hauled hay, hoed, picked cotton, and milked the cows at the Grady County farm. My brothers, just older and younger than me, were assigned to milk the cow at our new place in Lincoln County. So while I missed out on milking cows, driving tractors, and learning to repair them, my jobs were focused on harvesting, preserving, and cooking the food. I was primarily my mother's extra hand. Little did I know those tractor-driving skills I missed out on would come in handy twenty-five years later. How surprised would my father have been to see his least likely child dive into farming? His early death at fifty-eight years (when I was twenty-eight), before I started this journey, deprived both of us of that bond we could have created.

My two older sisters went to Oklahoma State University (OSU), where my brothers and I would eventually follow. Ahead of me were prospects of all the excitement new things offer, like Goldilocks investigating the home of the three bears. Throwing open all the possibilities of adventure and learning in a new environment, even for a nerd like me, was very seductive. With older siblings in education, microbiology, and biochemistry, and with my love of the out-of-doors, the sciences seemed a natural pathway for my higher education. I worked part-time in a biochemistry lab, and that seemed as good a major as any for someone who wasn't sure what she wanted to be when she grew up.

Looking back at that time, I realize I was slow to catch on to hints of my own interests and passions or the possibilities that exceeded my limited exposure. On my way to classes I walked many times past a greenhouse, curious about what was going on inside, but I never explored it. While botany was my favorite freshman course, I was bewildered when my fellow classmate and good friend from high school (a business major) hated it. But I never considered it a major. I had enough curiosity about all topics and just enough smarts that even genetics, chemistry, physics, and calculus kept my attention. I loved all learning and even took psychology as an elective on a whim— a whim that would change my life. The person teaching that class was my future husband.

How can I describe the impact meeting John Tedesco had on my life, this graduate student psychology teacher who became my life partner? He was able to stretch my world beyond the 160-acre farm, the small-town social life, the lack of expressed emotion in my family. How was I able to leave my early life in the rearview mirror and marry John seven months after our first date, to live beyond the borders of Oklahoma, first in Colorado, then Virginia before coming back to the Upper Midwest and John's home state of Iowa? He gave me the courage and support to move my life in those and future new directions, and the gift to be a stay-at-home mom with our two daughters. Because he was a child psychologist, he valued stay-at-home parenting.

After finishing my degree in chemistry in 1971 at our archrival University of Oklahoma (OU), I did not find inspiration in my chosen field. Failing to find a program in biochemistry there, my degree changed to chemistry. Leaving "bio" or life out of my last year of study did not match my interests as closely. For several years I worked in laboratories pushing test tubes, but it was just a job to meet our needs. Missing for me were the bigger picture, the higher purpose, the integration of ideas with results in an applied setting. What were my hobbies at the time that did inspire me? Gardening, of course. As soon as we owned our own home with a yard, there were gardens—a community plot in Virginia, and backyard plots in Iowa for every home we lived in. This helped me connect with what I not only wanted to preserve from the past, but needed—access to Nature. Having children added to what was really important. What was I going to feed them that contributed to their health and well-being?

This need to grow things went beyond just an appreciation for the taste of good food that I grew up having. It was a very real need to ground me, to connect with the spiritual dimension of life in the most profound way that I could. I needed to nurture life in the soil, observe and learn from it, and consume it directly. But it took years for me to realize that. Leaving my rural roots and living in urban areas, I needed to take vacations in the out-of-doors until such time that we landed on an acreage in a parklike setting, and then those urges subsided.

Viewing from afar with more wisdom, I can see that the sciences were leaving out important parts of the picture of life. Dissecting a frog in biology class led me to understand that that small creature was more than the sum of its parts under my knife. The food in the grocery stores that was grown by conventional agriculture was not producing the same product as the sacred love of life did in the garden for me. That call to my spiritual side eventually gave me confidence to take a job at our church as director of religious education. It gave me permission to stick my nose in books again to explore this spiritual side of myself and the world.

Who Speaks for Wolf by Paula Underwood was a book we used in our church school that was special to me. It spoke of the reverent consideration of all life before making a decision that would affect those and other lives. In the book an entire Native American village decides to relocate for better resources. At their planning meeting, tribal member Who Speaks for Wolf is not present. The rest of the members decide where to relocate without his input. This decision turns out to be a big mistake because the village is now in the path of a wolf pack habitat. The wolves became an irritation to the village. What was supposed to be an improvement had not worked because all the ramifications had not been considered. The story resonated with my belief that we should make decisions based on inherent wisdom of what is good for the whole rather than cater to whims and addictions or financial gains of the few. This could apply to everything from family life to politics.

Agriculture in particular stood out for me. Pesticide use was growing, government farm policies encouraged mono-cropping, and genetic engineering was the latest panacea. In 1984 the world had witnessed the deadly leak from a Union Carbide plant in Bhopal, India, of methyl isocyanate, a chemical used to make pesticides, which killed an estimated fifteen thousand people. Other environmental disasters were occurring, from the radioactive nuclear reactor accident in Chernobyl in 1986 to the *Valdez* oil spill in 1989. I wanted to make choices based on what would be best for the common good of people and the environment, and farming was where I could make a difference. Everyone eats. I wanted to grow food that was as good for people as it was for the environment.

My restless forays beyond our urban home as religious education director of our church were a search for something beyond the formal science world. But like Goldilocks, I still was not comfortable with where I had landed. I needed to do something with plants. It almost felt like "a calling." They gave me comfort, inspiration, and an endless opportunity to discover the mysteries and intricacies of life. The nudging had only taken twenty years since I had walked by that greenhouse on the OSU campus.

In 1992 I left the religious education job to attend Iowa State University for a degree in horticulture. While back at school, my real liberation came in finding others who were feeling the same lack in the agricultural system. We were wary, frustrated, and tired of a developing food system that treated the environment as a resource to be exploited and treated food crops as a commodity. These were not necessarily the university staff, but rather other students and committed individuals who were looking for new ways (or should I say improved old ways) to grow things, to serve community, and to honor farming, the soil, and our food.

With my rural farm roots sprouting anew, I finished a master's degree in horticulture in 1995. I then had the confidence to move forward with all the basic knowledge I had been collecting from my chemistry and graduate horticulture degrees, which included practical research on the land that I could continue to use. I felt inspired to start a small, organic farm and liked the cooperative nature of CSAs that I had learned about through extracurricular workshops and conferences. I had finally found a balance from the pendulum that swung from the farm to science to religion and back with my feet squarely planted in the soil. So here I found myself living that trite expression, coming full circle, back to farming, where I least expected to find myself. And Goldilocks found it just right.

My farm was not a manicured farm, but a working farm. Beautification was lower on the list of jobs than things more crucial to plant survival and production—planting, weeding, irrigating, and harvesting. I might not get the field edges mowed or every weed eliminated. I lost crops for a variety of reasons—weather, disease, weeds. A more experienced farmer perhaps could have prevented these occurrences. I tried not to dwell on the negatives, but sometimes had to remind people of the consequences of what had happened earlier in the season. The timing and rhythms of Nature proceed, stopping for no one, and they affect later harvests (or absence of harvest), which some customers tended to forget about after a month or two. In June when there were none of their favorite strawberries, I reminded them of the May frost when the strawberries were blooming and how that destroyed the fruit potential. But I also harvested an amazing bounty of food for hundreds of families from tiny seeds. That miracle of life can make anyone look good.

Of course, obstacles came along the way. People's ignorance bordered on being the largest. Once I was guiding a young woman from a large urban area around my organic farm. She seemed only vaguely interested as I explained the crops, cover crops, and fertility methods. At one point she stopped and looked down at the ground.

"ANTS! How do you kill ants?" she asked. She pointed to the insects on the ground busily doing their work.

"I . . . I don't," I replied, stunned that her only question of the tour was about how to rid the earth of a perceived annoyance. I did not take the opportunity at that time to explain how important ants are to the ecosystem. They aerate the soil with their tunnels and infiltrate nutrients when they take organic matter into those tunnels, similar to the work that earthworms do. Ants can pollinate certain flowers and eradicate some insect pests. I realized at that moment that it would take more than a leisurely stroll around the farm to educate some people about their food system.

My adventures of becoming a farmer on a piece of land in Iowa from 1995 through 2012 are the inspiration for this book. Turtle Farm was one of the first CSAs in Iowa. The farm served to educate a community of people—the farmers, the CSA customers, and many visitors. Just as the farm was transformed for food production by our well-intentioned actions, it worked to transform all those in touch with it by responding in turn. This is illustrated even further by a network of farmers, consumers, and sustainable agriculture advocates across the Upper Midwest and beyond who have found a special connection to the land and their food. Weather, insects, and animals were constant companions and challenges on the farm. I did research projects on site that directly impacted the farm in a practical way and that furthered my education and improved my production practices. When my own health crisis occurred, the farm became a guide for my healing. Land transfer was a difficult decision to address upon my retirement.

The second part of the book features recipes that I created or adapted, or were created by my customers who were inspired by the vegetable and fruit harvests. My favorite vegetable and fruit varieties, tips for speedy cooking, and stories about the food appear with the recipes.

May this book help transport you to the site of where your food is or could be grown, whether it be one or twenty acres, and to realize how adventurous a journey that food has endured to reach your plate.

Part I
Planting

1

A DELICIOUS REVOLUTION

Simply saying "I'm going to make a choice about the way I eat." This is a giant step . . . This decision can send you down a beautiful path—a delicious revolution.

—ALICE WATERS in *Hope's Edge,* by Frances Moore Lappé and Anna Lappé

WHEN I WAS FIRST LEARNING about community-supported agriculture (CSA), I saw the film *It's Not Just about Vegetables.* It explained that CSA farming is about more than the food. It's about healthy people and communities; it's about economics; it's about responsibilities; it's about connecting to the earth and changing perspectives. When farmers and customers create or join a CSA they have dared to follow a different path from a more conventional agriculture system guided by economic principles of bigger, cheaper, and more competitive. When we choose different values to guide us, we *are* a part of what Alice Waters calls a "delicious revolution."

CSAs were created to connect people with their food at the source—the farmer working the land. What struck me and many other farmers who embraced this new concept was the advantages it held for everyone involved. Farmers knew how many people to grow for, received payments up front to bridge the financial gap, and had season-long commitments relieving the pressure to continually market their crops. Customers not only received the freshest food available, but also had access to a farm they could call their own and visit. They could see how their food was being grown and learned more than they ever expected about their food. The land was being treated with respect, which for some was more important than the food being produced. We were all instilling our values into this process.

Once I began CSA farming, I considered my customers a bit like surrogate parents. They had helped seed the energy of the CSA partnership. Those seeds of intent were just as important as the physical seeds that would become the harvest of the season. What was it like to farm vegetables for CSAs? How does one get from seed to plate in this system? For me there was no greater job than getting to dream up a delectable farm plan and see it come into fruition. It wasn't unlike birthing a baby. Each season had a distinct personality. None was ever the same. Crops had different needs that had to be tended. As a farmer, I supported their growth and maturation, but the wider community was necessary as well for balanced success.

My goal was to grow the healthiest, tastiest, freshest, widest variety of food for my CSA that I could, to introduce customers to new vegetables or ways of using them, and to educate them to the cycles and intricacies of nature. I didn't guarantee that it would be easy or that there would not be bumps along the way. Each winter that I sat with clean nails awaiting a new growing season, I was ready to make a leap into that dream season on paper. I only hoped the weather, insects, farm helpers, and customers would throw out a safety net to cushion the landing.

Beginnings

You might think the farming starts when you set foot on the soil and begin to plant seeds there. For the wise, seasoned farmers, planning and implementation begin long before that. My physical crop planting began the previous October with the sowing of garlic cloves that would winter over, sprout new green growth in the spring, and be harvested the following July. Or one might say the farm plan started the previous March when I planted cover (or green manure) crops as natural fertilizers to prepare the soil for the next year. Sometimes those observations began before a seed even got into the ground. Mental notes sometimes made it on paper but often were just internal memos. Sometimes success involved new or improved equipment. Often it involved the timing of planting or anticipating weather and insects on the fly.

When the calendar turned to January, I had to set aside the colorful, enticing seed catalogs, tabulate the previous year's inventory of remaining seeds, and make final decisions. What variety of vegetables would fill the boxes all season long? How many people would I plan to grow for? Seed orders needed to be mailed in multiple catalogs before they ran out of stock. I had to create schedules for planting seeds in the field and transplants in the greenhouse. Greenhouse planting began in late January or early February, the same time I recruited and signed up customers for the CSA, got paperwork for organic certification prepared and submitted, ordered new tools or equipment, and found labor for the season. Winter was often the season for agricultural conferences when farmers had more time to be away from the farm. My favorite wintertime job was the greenhouse work. This started in the heated glass greenhouse at my home. Nothing cheered me up during the cold, dreary winters more than a sunny day planting seeds in the greenhouse. Often farm employees Sue Forrester and Ben Saunders would come over to help.

Sue came to the farm right after she moved to Iowa from Georgia. On the flight to her new home she had read a magazine article about CSAs. Her next-door neighbor was one of my Turtle Farm customers. Soon she called me to ask about working on the farm. She loved being outdoors, although she wasn't as fond of the wildlife. She had been known to abdicate picking certain sections of the asparagus patch to others after spotting snakes there. Sue loved to cook, and our conversations frequently were about food—what else! She was short in stature, but she was a real dynamo and a reliable worker. I admired that she spoke her mind.

Ben had started working for me after he finished his degree in horticulture at Iowa State University (ISU). At six-foot-three with a large frame, he was a foot taller than Sue. He sported a bushy beard and a thin ponytail down his back and was rarely seen in the winter without a knit cap, indoors or out. He had uncanny natural observation skills that surpassed mine whether it was in discovering insects feasting on our crops or a hawk's nest in a giant cottonwood at the farm. He also had great interest in becoming a vegetable farmer, so he asked many questions as we worked together.

Ben, Sue, and I were in the greenhouse surrounded by packets of seeds, stacks of empty flats, and potting soil (called media). "We're starting out with onions," I told my helpers. "We'll need ten flats of 'Ailsa Craig', the sweet onions, four seeds per cell, and then follow with ten flats of the scallions 'Evergreen Hardy', eight seeds per cell. We'll be lucky to get through that today. We'll do storage onions next time." These two onions not only led off the seeding in the greenhouse, they were the first onions to appear in the CSA boxes. 'Ailsa Craig' onions are mild enough to eat raw, though they are not as sweet as the more famous Georgia 'Vidalia' onions grown in the South or the 'Walla Walla' onions more commonly grown in the Northwest. They sized up quickly into beautiful, large teardrop onions. The spicy 'Evergreen Hardy' scallions have long sturdy leaves. The storage onions with their thin necks that dried down into a good seal for keeping longer term wouldn't be harvested until July or August. Some vegetable farmers prefer using onion sets (small bulbs planted in the ground that become larger onions) or onion transplants that can be purchased in the spring so that they do not have to grow their own. I found the sets produced smaller and lower quality onions, and certified organic transplants were hard to find and had fewer varietal choices than were available in seeds.

I filled the flats with the dark brown, fluffy potting soil, tapping the flat to settle it. Then I added more where the cells were not quite filled. Sue and Ben seeded flat after flat of the black seeds onto black media in a precise pattern. We would eventually fill the fourteen-by-twenty-foot greenhouse with planted flats of alliums (onion families)—leeks and shallots in addition to scallions and sweet and storage onions. The first group of allium flats would have to be moved outside to unheated cold frames about a month later so that we could fill the greenhouse up again with other cold-weather crops like lettuces, cabbages, broccolis, and kohlrabies. All this was before we even set foot in the field. Eventually we would fill the greenhouse a third time with warm-weather crops—tomatoes, peppers, eggplant, herbs, and more lettuces for succession planting.

As Turtle Farm CSA grew from 30 shares the first season to up to 180 shares in later years, so did the space needed for growing crops in the field and transplants in the greenhouse. I could expand the outdoor space easily as I was only using several acres of a twenty-acre farm. Greenhouse space, however, was limited. I had already increased that space after initially using the sunroom of our home for transplant production. My husband and I missed the use of that part of our house, so we built the glass greenhouse in our backyard. When that space began to be confining, I searched around for methods to use instead of building another structure.

One idea that I gleaned from *The New Organic Grower* by Eliot Coleman (1995) was to plant multiple seeds (four for onions) in growing medium rather than just one seed at a time. This would quadruple the number of onions in the same amount of space in a flat and would be a more efficient use of labor. I also compressed the size of the transplant soil ball that he used by half. I wanted to know if I could make these adjustments to Coleman's method and be successful in maintaining yield and reducing labor. At that time, I was a member of Practical Farmers of Iowa (PFI), an organization that sponsored on-farm research. PFI agreed to support my investigation comparing the two methods. Results showed that multiple-seeded onions yielded as well as or better than single-seeded onions, and labor savings were also higher in multiple-seed planting. After this research I continued to use multiple-seeded onion transplants with good success.

Sue, Ben, and I had not seen much of one another since the previous October. It was sunny, and that made the greenhouse quite warm and cozy. National Public Radio chattered to us in the background. Outside there were six

inches of snow on the ground. "Check out the deer," Ben
said, looking up from his work. Deer were filing past one
by one just outside the eight-foot fence my husband John
and I had recently constructed around our yard. "They
want to be in your yard eating your shrubbery, Angela. I've
counted ten so far."

"I'm glad to see the fence is doing its job," I replied hap-
pily. "Doesn't seem like they're as happy about it as I am."
The deer proceeded single file. They would cautiously stop,
raise their heads, flick their furry ears, and look at us,
noticing the motion in the greenhouse, then continue on.
Our home was located on a wooded acreage near a greenbelt around a lake. All wildlife was plentiful here. "That's
number twenty-three," I said as the last of the deer wan-
dered by. "Boy, am I glad we put up that fence." There were
occasional deer at the farm as well, and they often shared
in our harvests there. I debated the value of putting up a
fence at the farm but opted for other physical barriers to
protect the crops—mainly bird netting over hoops—that
were generally successful.

The actual turning of the soil in the spring marked the
mobilization of many plans. It was a relief when it could
be done once the weather was warm enough and the soil
had dried out enough to till. Planting jobs could stack up
on the schedule like pancakes if it was a particularly wet
spring, but once the garden was tilled, it was a great relief
to mobilize. Before I had my own tiller, finding someone
who could come and do the job took extra time and scheduling. I had asked around for someone who could till my
rented parcel and was given the name of Garland Duff. I
gave him a call, and he showed up the beginning of April
1996 when the land had dried out enough.

"Mr. Duff?" I asked of the older man who had driven up

in a spotless pickup truck with a trailer attached. On the trailer was a clean, bright green John Deere tractor with a tiller attached.

"That's right," he said with a raspy voice and a big grin. As he stepped out of his pickup I could see that he was stout and short in stature. He wore blue jeans supported by bright yellow suspenders with a plaid flannel shirt underneath. A miniature collie jumped out of the truck. "And this is Lassie. She goes everywhere with me." I would later find out that that meant even when he was on the tractor. They spent hours together that way.

We surveyed the two-acre site for tilling. "Well, let's check the soil to make sure it's not too wet to till," he said scooping up a handful of dirt. He squeezed the soil in his hand and then opened his fist to see if the dirt would retain its shape or crumble without much effort. The soil ball easily broke apart. I was happy to see him conduct this little test, which I used too. All it takes is one time of tilling soil that is too wet to learn that it delivers rock-hard clods of dirt that won't produce good crops. These clods don't break down until another winter freezes and thaws to cure the mistake. "I think that'll be fine," he said. "You know I'm eighty-two years young and still get around a lot to do this tilling. Lots of people need me for this. I got a brand new tractor this year." He was quite proud of his work, his equipment, and his age. For the next six years Garland would till my farm in the spring. I couldn't have had a more eager and cheerful helper in those early years.

Whether the tilling of the soil in the spring got done on schedule or not, the asparagus would break through the ground when it was ready, according to its own schedule. Asparagus is a perennial crop that comes up when the soil is warm enough to spur its growth; it was always the first vegetable delivered to customers. It often needed its own delivery schedule as there were no other crops ready at that time in April. But even if they were only getting a pound of asparagus, most customers couldn't wait to taste the initiation of the season. Except for maybe strawberries and tomatoes, it was the most eagerly anticipated crop that I grew.

Spring

During the spring season when we were frantically trying to get the majority of the thirty-plus types of crops planted, picking the asparagus every day, wrestling with irrigation lines, even weeding here and there, it would almost be irritating to have to stop this frenzy to start harvesting vegetables for the May deliveries. Of course, it was the point of the whole process—getting the food to the customers. But spring inevitably provided the best weather for planting and weeding on harvest days. Or conversely it might rain on harvest days and make it difficult to do weeding and planting the next day. Call it a farmer's version of Murphy's Law. And that law wasn't limited just to us; it could affect farmers everywhere. I once received a phone call from a farmer in Oregon who had been contracted to ship organic asparagus roots to customers like me who had ordered them from a certain seed company.

"Hi! Have you planted your asparagus roots yet?" he asked.

"Well, yes, we got all fifteen hundred of them in last week just ahead of a nice rain. It was perfect timing. They went in really well," I said. "Why do you ask?"

"Well, I sent the wrong variety to you. I was supposed to send 'Jersey Giant', but I sent 'UC157' instead," he said.

"You sent the wrong variety?" I repeated slowly, hoping in the back of my mind that maybe this was a joke.

"Yeah, I got my farm map turned upside down and dug the wrong patch," he said rather sadly. "I was wondering if you still wanted me to send the correct variety or if you would be okay with the 'UC157'. It's the most popular variety in California," he continued. I could feel an edge of pleading in his voice. This was no joke!

I felt put on the spot to make a decision. I wasn't happy at all about the switch. My customers and I loved the flavor of the 'Jersey Giant'. "Let me think about it, and I'll get back to you," I said to buy some time. What kind of variety only had initials and numbers for a name? Most likely a research variety, I assumed. Some data I found said 'UC157' did not produce as well in the Midwest as 'Jersey Giant' did. But just as important to me was the fact that I didn't know what 'UC157' tasted like. Flavor is hugely important to CSA crops. It does no good to find vigorous, productive varieties if they don't appeal to the taste buds and don't get eaten. I had long ago learned that beauty or productivity do not always translate into good flavor. Asparagus is a long-term crop that can produce well for a dozen years or more. I didn't want to invest in something I might not be happy with. I called the farmer back and asked him to send me the correct variety. Luckily, he didn't want his 'UC157' roots back.

At other times, just when a Murphy's Law disaster seemed a poor decision away, we seemed to have Nature's luck on our side. One year we were about to plant sweet potatoes on a single day in June. We'd already held them a week past their arrival date because we were so busy with harvests and other jobs around the farm. June was already late in the season to plant them, and that day it was hot, dry, sunny, and very windy; not good conditions for putting out little plants with hardly any roots to find moisture. Many plants put in the ground under such conditions would wave goodbye before the day was over. But if we didn't plant them that day, we wouldn't have enough time or workers for another week to do it. As late in the day as we could wait to spare them hours of parching sun, we planted the sweet potatoes—1,200 little slips of stem with maybe a leaf or two, a few hairy roots on the end with no soil attached. Then we laid out trickle irrigation lines to give them a drink. When we left that evening, they looked like they were on death's door, wilted and drooping. The next morning, I drove slowly onto the farm and held my breath as I passed the rows so that I could check on their status. From my truck I could see that the sweet potatoes had perked up and were growing! Sweet potatoes are amazingly resilient plants. But don't try this in your garden with just any bare root transplant.

One spring dilemma that we watched for was a late frost. If you get too impatient and plant tender crops such as tomatoes and peppers too early, you could easily lose them to frost. Replacing them would be nearly impossible at that late a date. Organic transplants were not easily found, and if you should be lucky enough to find someone growing them, purchasing them could be a major blow to your budget, especially after having already spent the time and money to grow your own. One year when we planted part of our 1,300 tomato transplants a week after the "last frost free date for Iowa," we heard the forecast for an upcoming frost. Rather than take a chance on losing half of the crop, we pulled all those first transplants, and then planted them again when the forecast was "safe."

We might lose any asparagus spears above ground to frost, but it does not affect the plants otherwise. New spears will grow up in a few days. Our biggest concern with a late frost was flowering strawberries. We generally raked the winter blanket of straw mulch off the strawberries in mid-April, or when we could see some growth in the dormant plants. The timing of mulch removal would then have an effect on when the plants greened up and, about a month later, bloomed. Open blossoms were vulnerable to injury. Blossoms that had not yet opened or had already transformed to berries were usually safe. Sometimes we could cover the strawberries with huge pieces of thin polyester fabric to protect them and other times not. Overhead sprinklers are a preferred way to protect strawberries from frost, but we didn't have an overhead system in place and used trickle irrigation instead.

Sometimes customers with their own strawberry patches in their home gardens would ask me why they might have a year with no fruit. Frost can spoil your strawberry crop without you noticing if you are not attuned to the signs. It can frost even though the temperature may not get down to thirty-two degrees. If your berries are in bloom when there is a frost warning, especially if the dew point will hover near freezing, cover them with blankets or pull the straw you may have had them covered with over the winter back over the plants. If you notice your strawberry flowers have black spots in their yellow centers several days later, they have been damaged by frost and those flowers will not produce berries.

Summer

By the time summer arrives mid-June, most farm activities have settled into a routine. Tuesdays and Fridays were harvest and delivery days. Harvesting might also take place on other days depending on how often a crop may need picking. Okra, summer squash, and cucumbers grew so quickly they needed picking every other day. Temperatures can also make a difference. Strawberries and raspberries could use picking every other day if it was warm and sunny, but if weather turned cooler, they could often wait another day and not be past peak ripeness. Harvesting on delivery days involved picking crops from early morning until noon. After lunch we cleaned the vegetables and packed the boxes. They were off to CSA pickup sites within hours of growing in the garden.

The location of Turtle Farm twenty miles from the heart of Des Moines meant we were one of the closest farms for urban folks to visit. We often got free publicity from these visits as well as some satisfaction of helping educate the public. CSAs were such a new concept at the time, the more word that got out about them the better it would be for us and other CSA farms. Farms less interested in the community aspect might think these visits were just taking up the farmer's valuable time (and they did), but when we could, we promoted this philosophical aspect of this revolutionary farming concept; it was just one more piece of the cooperative model we aspired to.

A nearby community college that had horticulture classes would bring students several times a year to visit the farm. Turtle Farm was only thirty miles from ISU, making it a favorite site for teachers and researchers to visit. Frequently researchers needed an organic farm to contrast with conventional methods for their research experiments. Des Moines is a hub of magazine publishing. On more than one occasion, people working on stories about vegetables would want to visit and take pictures at the farm, and over the years we were featured in *Gardening Ideas*, *Outdoor Living*, and *Better Homes and Gardens*. The word about CSAs was getting out!

One year we had Ken Gill, the owner of some beautiful draft horses, come and pull an antique plow during the potato harvest. We made it a day for the CSA customers to visit the farm and participate. Activities like this that we could share with our community benefited us all. Besides being educational, they gave some ownership and appreciation of the farm to the customers. Many children (and even some adults) do not know how crops grow or are harvested. Ken's two large golden-colored horses were well trained and beautiful to watch. "BACK, BACK," Ken said clearly and slowly as he urged them one at a time to back out of their trailer. It was a misty, foggy morning. Ben and I scurried to the barn to bring crates and small buckets to the potato patch. "Here, want a bucket to hold your potatoes?" I asked the grandchild of one of my customers. Her eyes lit up as she eagerly took the small, white bucket.

Ken hooked the calm horses to the plow and lined them up with a row of withered potato vines. He got onto the rusty seat of the plow and called out, "Betsy, Jess, WALK." The horses' muscled shoulders leaned forward as their feet pushed against the ground. Their majestic heads bobbed up and down with their steps. The shovel of the plow slid into the soil, and the dirt moved up to a conveyer belt with spacers. The belt was driven by the turning wheels of the plow, and the soil began falling away from the potatoes and through the spacers. The potatoes landed gently atop the overturned earth. As the plow got to the end of the row, Ken called out, "WHOA, GEE." The horses stopped and then slowly turned to line up with the next row.

The crowd of adults and children that had gathered were mesmerized by the process. It was one of those magical moments when we gave volunteers the opportunity to help with the farm tasks. They jumped forward to pluck the potatoes out of the disturbed black soil, place them in their buckets, and then empty them into our crates. One adult customer, Cece, came up to me laughing and said, "I almost knocked over that little kid, I got so excited to grab the potatoes."

The farm crew and I were always learning from my diverse employees. I had nutritionists and dieticians explain plants' nutritional properties, an entomologist and amateur herpetologist taught me insect and snake identifications and benefits, and other horticulturists, who had learned different facts than I had in school, expanded my knowledge base in different years. Molli Moody had worked for me one summer when she was a student in agriculture at ISU. She was tall, solid, and had a mischievous streak that intimidated the two husky young men who worked for me the same season. Sometimes she wore an ISU T-shirt that said, "Where would you be without agriculture?" on the front. The back read, "Naked and hungry." That fall she had left to serve in Iraq as a member of the army reserves. We were sad to see her go and wished her well during her service overseas. She came back to work the next season, but still had some annual duties as a member of the reserves.

"Angela, I have to be gone three weeks in June this year for my reserve training," she told me at the beginning of the season in May.

I looked at the calendar with her dates marked out. "Great," I said sarcastically. "You do realize that's high strawberry season." The farm was especially busy when we had to pick strawberries in addition to all the other chores. Molli was a good worker, so I would deal with her absence by hiring more temporary berry pickers.

When Molli returned from her professional duties that summer, she announced she had a treat for us. "Tomorrow lunch is on me," she said, with a twinkle in her eye. There weren't many options for lunch in the small, rural community of Granger where the farm was located, so we typically brought our own food—anything from peanut butter and jalapeño sandwiches to leftovers from a gourmet meal.

The next day at lunch time, Molli retrieved a large sack from her truck. "What are we having?" Sue eagerly asked. Lunch was always a big deal for the hungry, tired farm crew.

"Lunch is MREs," she replied. Molli had brought the packaged army "meals ready to eat" for us to sample. "I've got one for each of you, and they're all different. This is what I've lived on for the past three weeks and, of course, in Iraq before that."

"Well, this will be different. I've never had or even seen one of these," I said looking over my rations in the metal container. "I've got Menu No. 5—grilled chicken. For such a small packet, there's a lot packed in here." I read off the items, "Chicken breast fillet, seasoned, filled, chunked and formed; minestrone stew; wheat snack bread; cheese spread with jalapeños; almond poppy seed pound cake; packet of M&Ms; French vanilla cappuccino powder; iced tea drink mix; jalapeño ketchup; salt; 2 Chiclets gum pieces; plastic spoon; moist towelette; and a tiny packet of toilet paper. Wow! That's a lot of food with a few extras to boot."

We each spread out our food. The meals even came with little heaters that were activated by a chemical substance when you added water. I used it to heat my chicken and minestrone. The heater got so hot it smoked. Also enclosed was a plastic bag to heat water for the drink mixes. None of us finished our meals. They were intended to be high performance meals providing 1,200 to 1,300 calories for active duty.

"Well, I like certain parts better than others," Sue said after finishing her meal.

"Believe me, it's the same for the military," Molli added. "We all have favorite menus that we fight for, but we even get tired of those after a while."

"It makes me appreciate our fresh veggies even more," I said. "There weren't many included unless you count the ketchup and jalapeños."

The contrast couldn't be more glaring. Here was a meal compressed into a metal container that was fuel for the military, most likely scientifically determined in a laboratory to provide ample calories, storability, and efficiency in times of duress. Surrounding us as we ate were fields of living, green, growing plants filled with vital nutrients the body needed. Survive versus thrive seemed to sum up the difference for me. MREs were almost the antithesis of what we were doing nurturing the soil and plants to produce the healthiest food we could for our customers.

Late summer often found many personnel changes. One of the nicest things about Sue, as a stay-at-home mom who worked for me for eight years, was that she was available early and late in the season when others might not be. Students, who generally made up the majority of my employees, often couldn't start work until mid-May and needed to get back to school by mid-August. The workload on the farm did not necessarily change to accommodate those situations. It usually meant that by the end of August into September we only had time to harvest crops continuously. No weeding and very little planting would be taking place at that time. But the warm-weather crops were still going strong while the fall crops of winter squashes, greens, and sweet potatoes were waiting in the wings. It was enough to make us remaining workers wish for the deer and rabbits to visit and lessen our workload.

Fall

Aahhh! The fall crops—the patiently waiting leeks, winter squashes, and sweet potatoes, perhaps a few remaining potatoes, a return of turnips, radishes, lettuce, and spinach. The heat-loving tomatoes, peppers, eggplant, and green beans were waning. Days were shorter, and there came a tinge of crispness in the air. There was something calming about the season and the crops. They seemed quiet and unassuming. And it was a good thing, for I was weary physically and emotionally from the demands of the harvest. As much as I loved this job and couldn't think of anything I would rather be doing, the end of the season could never arrive soon enough. I wondered how farmers with animals who do not get the winter break from daily chores managed. Certainly vegetable and fruit farming, especially CSA farming where there can be so many crops to manage (we had more than thirty types of vegetables and hundreds of varieties), was more intense through the entire growing season than row-crop or animal farming, but we did get the winters off—at least if we so chose. More and more vegetable farmers are now extending their season through the use of hoop houses or refrigerated or dry storage crops that can be sold past the outdoor growing season.

Fall crops can be large. White, sturdy daikon radishes with their green frilly leaves could be measured in feet. The beautiful round leaves of collard greens would outsize a dinner plate. A head of 'Late Flat Dutch' cabbage made eye-popping growth worthy of *Ripley's Believe It or Not*. Sweet potatoes the size of footballs were fun to dig if you didn't stab them first with the spading fork. 'Amish Pie' pumpkins were so large and thick-skinned that customers had trouble carving into them. One enterprising customer resorted to dropping hers on concrete to crack it open.

The changing seasons were demonstrated daily on the farm. By late summer and fall the birds were not nearly as active. The tree leaves were starting to color and drop. The dusty corn and soybean harvests buzzed all around us sending up thick, brown clouds. And then there were the migrating birds. White pelicans appeared at a nearby lake in the spring and fall on their migration route. They stayed as long as a month or more each time. Some days they would soar silently overhead, strengthening their wings for their continued long journey ahead. We would stretch and rest our weary backs and give them a reverent audience.

When frost took the garden (usually the first week of October), the harvest of many crops ended. The tomatoes, peppers, eggplant, and any remaining basil were all silent, blackened victims. Crops remaining that were cold and frost tolerant occupied the October share: radishes, beets, turnips, spinach, lettuce, cabbages, broccoli, collards, kale, Brussels sprouts, and potatoes. The varieties of winter squashes were the stars this time of year as they had taken all season to mature, and they held up well in storage. The varieties seemed endless: 'Honey Bear' acorns, 'Sweet Dumpling' and 'Zeppelin' delicatas, butternuts, pumpkins, spaghetti squash, and on and on. And once that final harvest of these late crops was finished, a new series of tasks took place on and off the farm.

The fall rituals at season's end started with cleaning up the garden—cleaning tools, removing trickle irrigation lines from the crops, putting away tomato cages. We planted garlic for the next year. A delivery of several truckloads of straw bales would be used to mulch that garlic and the strawberries. Although I was happy to come to the end of the growing season (I could rest and read that stack of books that had accumulated over the summer), it was also a time of mourning. I'd miss the fresh, locally grown produce—the tomatoes, basil, and eggplant—friends that I wouldn't see until the following summer except perhaps in the freezer or a canning jar.

It was a time for reflection and evaluation of the season—what would we do differently next year? A survey went out to customers so that they could participate in that process. Did they get too much or too little of this or that vegetable? Were there glitches in the delivery process that needed correcting? Every season saw changes and improvements from this. And it was a time of celebration and thanksgiving. We held a potluck at the farm to encourage families to visit the farm again. They could see the earth laid bare of its bounty. Remnants of plants that had given their lives for our nourishment scattered the landscape. In stark contrast, inside the farm stand on the counters, beautiful and diverse food dishes were displayed—plants transformed into delicious edibles. It was good and complete.

"We want the recipes in the next newsletter, Angela," a customer requested.

"Can we glean?" another asked.

"Sure! Follow me, and I'll show you what's still left in the garden," I said as I grabbed my pruners and led them on a tour of secret places and their hidden, leftover gems that they could take home.

Gleaning, the practice on farms of collecting leftover food that might otherwise go to waste, has been practiced since biblical times as a way to feed the poor and hungry. Many farms have imperfect produce for which they have no market, so there is no point in expending the labor to pick it. CSAs distribute and share that extra produce in the weekly box. There were times when some crops were so abundant that we were afraid the customers might throw them back at us, like the year everyone got up to ten large cucumbers in their weekly box. That's one reason we had "put back" crates at the distribution sites. If a person did not like a vegetable or could not use the amounts given to them, they could put it back for others who might. We often had discussions as we packed the boxes on whether or not to put in a deformed, split, or imperfect item once the marketable ones were packed.

At every season's end I extended my heartfelt thanks to my cocreator customers and friends who had made this season possible. I would miss seeing them over the winter hibernation. They reminded me of lines in a Max Coots poem ("Let Us Give Thanks") that expresses thanks "for friends as unpretentious as cabbages, as subtle as summer squash, as persistent as parsley, as delightful as dill, endless as zucchini, and who, like parsnips, can be counted on to see you throughout the winter."

2

FINDING TURTLE FARM

We come and go, but the land is always here. And the
people who love it and understand it, are the people
who own it—for a little while.
—WILLA CATHER, *O Pioneers!*

LET'S TAKE A STEP BACK, and let me properly introduce
you to Turtle Farm. At twenty acres, it was but a speck of
real estate in the Upper Midwest, where farms more commonly measure in the hundreds or thousands of acres.
Those large farms grow primarily row crops of corn and
soybeans. Fruits and vegetables, the crops I grew for
community-supported agriculture (CSA), are high-value,
labor-intensive crops that can be profitable on as little as
five acres. But those smaller parcels are not plentiful, especially to buy. Through friends I initially found a two-acre
parcel for my first two years and a ten-acre parcel for the
third year, but both of those were short-term rentals. The
perennial fruits I intended to grow needed a more permanent location for their continued growth and production.
Strawberries and raspberries don't even produce the first
year you plant them. Blueberries or an orchard might take
five years. Even a five-year lease can seem short-term for an
investment in perennial crops and putting up greenhouses
or other needed infrastructure. Purchasing land would

ensure that any improvements or perennials planted could be for the long term. The first part of this farming adventure was to find appropriate land to purchase.

In 1988 my husband and I moved to an acreage in Johnston, Iowa, a suburb of Des Moines, on the edge of the Saylorville Lake greenbelt. In the middle of a state known for farm country, our spot in the shadow of the Des Moines River was a paradise for wildlife. We were frequently visited by deer, coyotes, wild turkeys, fox, and many magnificent birds—even eagles on occasion. Painted turtles made their homes in a pond across from the house and laid their eggs in our lawn each spring. Every time we started down the eighth-mile-long driveway to our home under a heavy canopy of trees, our cares and worries were swept aside like a meditative wash. But it was difficult to envision a farm here; two of our property's three acres were in woods and driveway. That left less than an acre at our home for growing purposes. We loved this peaceful, semiurban site, but we knew that it wouldn't be a good choice for my farming ambition.

While I was still in graduate school, John and I began the search elsewhere for farmland. After my graduation in 1995 when I began driving thirty minutes each day to my rented plot, we knew we had to find something closer, so that narrowed our search. There were lots of things to consider besides just distance. Zoning, access to nearby markets, availability of water, neighbors and their chemical usage, and affordability all mattered to me. Soil type was a high priority. In Iowa, farm ground is rated for its corn suitability rating (CSR) with higher numbers up to 100 indicating more valuable soil for that crop. Iowa State University created this measurement in 1971 (and updated it to CSR2 in 2013) to compare potential production of different soils for corn. The soil type, drainage, and slope of the land are some elements of that rating. Finding any farm that ticked all the boxes would have been a chore, but a *small* farm with all these characteristics was especially rare because most nearby farmland was sold in massive acreages for large commercial operations. The farm economy was good, and available land was often snatched up by current farmers expanding their acreages, causing land prices to increase.

Three years after leaving graduate school, I pulled my pickup to the side of the highway on the edge of Granger. Across the road was a property for sale—ninety-nine acres of bare ground. By this time I was thinking outside the box more and looking at larger properties. I scanned the boundaries and went through the list of requirements in my mind. More slope than I wanted, but not too much. A few trees good for birds, wildlife, and windbreak on the north side, but mostly tillable ground. There was great access to local markets on this state highway only twenty miles from the Des Moines metro area, but I knew that would make the lot more expensive. It was ten miles from our home, a fifteen-minute commute. Its CSR rating, which averaged 88 over different parts of the farm, was good. Okay overall, not perfect, but how long would it take to find perfection? Could this be a diamond in the rough? The real question was, would the owners split the land up and sell us a smaller parcel?

We called our realtor, Howard Elson. Howard was a patient man near retirement age who enjoyed looking at rural properties around Des Moines (though I think he was actually scouting good fishing holes in the process). He had grown up on a farm north of the city and was very familiar with the area. For three years, Howard, John, and I had scaled steep hills, cleared creeks, climbed over fences, and explored outbuildings and even homes on countless properties.

"I think you should buy forty acres," Howard said. The land that had caught my eye was easily accessible on a state highway, and there were no neighboring properties that drained onto it. This was important because improper drainage could contaminate organic ground with chemicals or animal manures. It had been farmed conventionally with chemicals so there would be a three-year waiting period without chemical use to get organic certification. The soil was light with more sand than clay—good for vegetable production. But the site was also in a prime area for future development, and its price reflected that.

"We were thinking more like twenty," I said. A larger purchase would have meant a bigger commission for Howard, but I knew he was thinking more about the potential of the land as an investment than his pocketbook. Land speculation was not an area we felt comfortable with. "Howard, I don't have any large equipment to take care of that much property, let alone afford it," I continued. John and I were cautious. There were so many unknowns. I didn't have experience growing for profit yet. In farming, big ideas don't always guarantee success, especially with the vagaries of weather, pests, and markets. Most farm families have off-farm income to survive these uncertainties. John would continue to provide our income. For that I was very privileged and grateful. I, at the very least, wanted to be able to use my profits to pay for the land. My farming adventure was requiring a large mortgage, and forty acres would double that payment.

"Well, you could always hire it done," Howard responded with optimism. We could see his wisdom but chose to stick with the twenty acres. Even at that size I would still have to hire out some of the work.

Holding our breath, we decided to move ahead with the property, and things fell into place, giving us confidence that this could work. Iowa at the time had a special program for women and minorities that reduced the loan interest for farm purchases, which we took advantage of. The Ritter family, who owned the property, graciously allowed me early access so that the farm crew and I could put in strawberries and raspberries to be ready for the following year. There was no entry to our twenty-acre parcel yet, so we entered the property on a small farm access drive near the remaining seventy-nine-acre parcel. We also carried five-gallon buckets of water to irrigate the berries by hand that summer. The following spring I arranged for a driveway to be put in and had a well drilled. Mr. Ritter put in a cover crop of alfalfa for me as the deal was being finalized. That fall of 1998 we became the proud yet apprehensive owners of twenty acres of fertile Iowa farm ground. We exhaled.

I knew little about this sleepy but growing town of Granger across the road from the farm and the surrounding community that we were now a part of. The 2000 census cited the population as 583. In 2010 it had grown to 1,244. I had traveled many times in the past on the two busy highways that intersected the town, but never stopped. Two of my future CSA customers lived there. As I approached Granger from the east on my way to the farm, cresting a hill, I could see two water towers looming over the town. Most small towns have only one. To take advantage of this curious anomaly, the town had painted one tower "hot" and the other "cold." Obviously the people of Granger had a sense of humor, and it helped me to start each day with a smile. I would slowly learn more details about the area and the people.

John and I had noticed when we were first exploring the farm that there was an abandoned railroad right-of-way on the southern edge of the ninety-nine-acre property. A refurbished train station still stood in the town, a testament to a busier time of people and crops using rail lines to reach markets in Des Moines. Semitrucks now replaced those trains. One of the prominent businesses in Granger was Barr-Nunn Trucking whose trucks we had often seen on Iowa's interstates. A few years later they would build a new headquarters directly across the road from the farm, and its owner would eventually buy the remaining seventy-nine acres of land that we did not purchase.

In addition to farmers' crops and people, some trains in the early 1900s also carried the circus! What a welcome distraction from everyday life that must have been for the people of Granger. I have not seen it but have learned that two miles southeast of Granger and the farm is an elephant graveyard, all that remains of the winter headquarters of Fred Buchanan's Circus, later called the Yankee Robinson Shows, the World Brothers Circus, and then Robbins Brothers Circus. Its demise came in the 1930s during the depression. My somewhat morbid (yet agricultural!) curiosity upon hearing this story led me to wonder whether elephant compost made things grow larger at that graveyard.

When I drove to the Casey's gas and convenience store in Granger, I would also pass by the Catholic Assumption Church and School. Later I would be contacted by a teacher there who requested that we have a children's garden on the farm for their preschoolers. This church had a huge impact on Granger when its priest Luigi Ligutti, who served from 1926 until 1940, helped the community take advantage of one of only thirty-four federal Division of Subsistence Homesteads—part of Roosevelt's New Deal programs to provide housing for lower-income people in 1933. This program settled fifty families on the western edge of Granger, an area that became known as Granger Homesteads. These small acreages with homes provided better self-sufficiency for families of seasonally employed miners who worked in the coal mines nearby. Eleanor Roosevelt visited in 1936 to honor Granger Homesteads as one of the most successful projects of the short-lived program.

When I stood at the top of the hill of Turtle Farm's new home that first year, and every other, the view to the west encompassed the entire town of Granger and was a constant reminder of that community. Under my feet were the remains of glaciers from the last ice age that gifted Iowa its fertile soils. Here once grew the tall grass prairies that built up the topsoil that I would be tending, or what remained of it. Farming during the past century had seriously eroded that base. Before the farming communities began, the Sauk and Meskwaki (Sac and Fox) and other Iowa Native American tribes roamed this area and called it home, at least until the Cession 262 Treaty removed them in 1840. Recognizing this complicated history that preceded me, I now carried a wealth of attachment and love for the land as others did before me.

~~~~~~~~~~~~

In the spring of 1999, I moved forward on improvements to the bare ground and proceeded with creating the treasure of a farm I had dreamt of. An entrance, driveway, and small parking area were installed. Drilling a well was a major investment, but a necessary one for growing vegetables, which themselves are 90 percent water. A friend who was retiring from farming sold me a used walk-in cooler to keep the perishable fruits and vegetables refrigerated. I put up a hoop house with the expectation of growing early crops in a protected environment. The hoop house was an unheated plastic greenhouse held up by a steel frame. Eventually as each spring seemed to bring warmer and warmer weather, we used it mainly for transplant production.

It would be several more years before I built a barn. Farm country abounds with Morton buildings, a company name that has become generic for metal-shelled structures on wooden frames that cover farm equipment and supplies. I was hoping for something more traditional and sturdy. Doug Nichols, the local carpenter I eventually hired to build my barn, was a superb choice. It was inspiring to watch him create our small masterpiece of board-and-batten style. He worked alone, but could still maneuver large boards up to the rafters. John made time to paint the barn for me. Soon the barn housed my tractor and other equipment, and it had a room for packing boxes that also served as the farm stand. A very important feature of that barn was a composting toilet. It was a good feeling to be past the days of needing to go to the city park or the nearby corn fields for toilet facilities.

The person I brought on to do some of my tractor work was Ray James. Ray was retired from a farm manufacturing business and knew all farm equipment inside and out. He kept busy on his small nearby farm, doing contract work baling hay. He loved his draft horses and eventually bought a carriage wagon to rent out for weddings and special events. While Ray loved his animals, he could be a bit crusty around people.

"You need to get those rocks out of that field before I break my equipment on them," Ray said gruffly to me one day. He was mowing the upper part of the farm that was in alfalfa. I wasn't sure how to deal with his attitude but needed his help, so I proceeded to do as he asked. After all, I was the beginner here. A helper and I hauled many wheelbarrows of rocks out of that field and brought them to the edge of the woods. Eventually Ray's softer side appeared. Several times he told us how hard we were working compared to some farmers chatting over coffee each morning at the local convenience store. Ray stopped by the farm often to chat, and his visits seemed to occur more frequently during strawberry season.

"Are the strawberries ripe yet?" he would ask, not only during the summer months, but any time of year. It became his standard greeting. Ray was crucial in helping me with the large equipment challenges of my early farming career. I may not always have been able to repair the used relics he found at the farm auctions, but I could always count on Ray. In some ways I think he filled a role that my father would have played had he been alive. Like Ray, my father could fix just about anything on a farm. Unlike Ray, my father would have done so in a much less chatty manner.

For the first few years, there was little to break the serenity of being on the farm except for the highway traffic on the western border. There was active farming on the north and south sides of the farm and pasture ground to the east. Amid casual conversation, the farm crew and I could hear the bird songs and the breezes rustling the plants. I knew that wouldn't last long because development was moving this way from Des Moines. The remaining seventy-nine acres that we didn't buy, which had been purchased by the owner of Barr-Nunn Trucking, had now been sold to a developer. A tract of houses was planned, giving us thirteen new neighbors directly abutting the farm and many more beyond.

And then it began. Huge earthmovers were brought in to begin working the soil. They were right next to the farm boundary with large engines roaring and making repetitive squeaking noises like giant hinges that needed oil. It was constant movement, constant noise. Besides the clatter that assaulted our ears, it was painful to see how destructive the development process was to the ground. The developer's first step was to remove and pile the valuable topsoil. The topsoil is where the majority of the soil community exists—microbes, bacteria, insects, earthworms, small rodents. Piling the soil eight to ten feet high drove out any oxygen that sustained that life in the soil. Then the subsoil and deeper layers were gouged, moved, and restructured to provide the base the developer wanted for infrastructure and home foundations. When the houses were finished, a thin layer of the topsoil was put back on the surrounding yard and the remainder sold. In Iowa this layer used to be set at a minimum of four inches, but the required depth has been changed to allow developers more leeway. The construction industry insisted it was too expensive to follow the previous rule. The farm's new neighbors who bought those homes had trouble growing gardens in their new yards without bringing in compost and more topsoil. The thin layer of topsoil the developer had left was not enough to absorb the water running across their lawns and creating small rivers in their backyards.

This lack of respect for the soil and the farm showed up on more than one occasion and almost all came as a result of the new housing development next door. I once found a load of construction debris and trash deliberately dumped where the street butted up against our land. The farm crew and I cleaned up truckloads of lightweight debris that blew onto the farm constantly when a house was under construction. Without our permission or advance knowledge a neighbor once used a skid loader to enter the farm to gain access to his backyard where he was doing some work. In the process he ran over one of our peach trees. "I'll replace your tree," he said offhandedly.

"Why did you bring the machine through the farm rather than your own property?" I demanded.

"Well, that lawn is sod, and this is just grass," he replied.

"If the farm was another lot with a house, what would you have done?" I pushed him further. His glazed expression told me I was getting nowhere. There was no recognition of the value of the farm ground.

On another occasion I arrived at the farm to see deep depressions across part of the cover crop field, obviously made by a large, heavily laden truck. As I visually followed the tracks, they led to one of the houses being constructed. I went to visit with the workers.

"What are you doing driving across my farm?" I challenged them.

"Our truck got stuck in the backyard, and it was the only way we could get out. Otherwise we would have had to call a tow truck," one of them responded. "You weren't here, so we couldn't ask permission."

I was so incredulous at his answer that I knew further discussion was useless. "Give me the name and number of your boss," I said.

When I reached their boss, she seemed genuinely upset with what her workers had done. "I grew up on a farm and can appreciate what they did was very inappropriate. What can I do to make up for it?" she asked.

"There's nothing anyone can do about those deep ruts. It will take years of winter's freeze-and-thaw cycles of the soil to repair the compaction. The oxygen loss in that soil will impact the growth of any crop for years," I explained. I was not happy to not ask for reparations, but I knew there was nothing physically that could be done. I then decided on a solution that would make me feel a little better. "You can make a donation to Practical Farmers of Iowa," I said. It was one of my favorite sustainable farming organizations. She did.

During my years caring for this piece of land, this base for my farming endeavors, I did my best to protect the soil and its inhabitants. I rotated crops to avoid disease. I planted cover crops to protect from wind and water erosion, including permanent barriers of grass or perennial crops across hillsides. I placed "Do Not Spray" signs at the highway so that the county would not spray pesticides on the property edges and endanger the organic certification that I received after the three-year waiting period. And the land responded in kind with bountiful harvests of many crops. The possibilities seemed endless. For me, for the others who helped me work its soil, and for the CSA consumers of its harvests, Turtle Farm became a polished gem that bound us together in a community with purpose and dedication. That purpose was growing healthy food in an ecologically viable manner, taking care of the land, and working in cooperation with Nature. Turtle Farm would lead us on a wonderful adventure.

3

FOOD AS SACRED

That's what the sacred is all about. It's not a concept but an experience—an experience of awe, of wonder, of beauty. And with the sacred comes the zeal, the energy.

—MATTHEW FOX, *Recapture the Sacred*

RED VANS MARKED "Des Moines Area Community College" turned off the highway onto the driveway of the farm. Numerous cars followed, their turn lights flashing. They parked haphazardly on the gravel parking area, up and onto the lawn, and near the field edges. Danielle Wirth stepped out of one of the vans and walked up to greet me, smiling widely. She was wearing her Turtle Farm T-shirt with tan slacks. Her wavy, long, honey-blonde hair was parted in the middle and hinted at her low-maintenance, natural look that only lacked a headband to place her as a hippie from the sixties.

Danielle, a former park ranger turned environmental science teacher, was taking her students on field trips to study farming practices that differed from large-scale, industrial agriculture—farms that acted in true part-nership with the Earth. Six months earlier Danielle had attended a gathering of new community-supported agri-culture (CSA) farmers, of which I was a part, who were looking for a different way of connecting with food and their customers—farmers who wanted to see the sanctity and respect for our planet and its fruits honored. Danielle was not a farmer herself, but she wanted to bring her environmental science class to visit our farms for their lab experience and to meet the farmers—to bring the textbooks and classroom lectures alive.

Students spilled out of the vans and cars. They carried spiral notebooks and chatted among themselves to puncture the quiet of this afternoon on the farm. Danielle had scheduled this visit so that the older students comprising part of her class could bring their families. The large urban setting of the Des Moines Community College encouraged and was convenient for participation of all ages. One girl tugged at her mother's arm to drag her toward the flowers in front of the barn. Grasshoppers scattered wildly at the intrusion. Another boy shyly hid behind his mother.

I greeted Danielle's students as they gathered in an amorphous group, led them out of the sun into the farm stand, and gave them an introduction to the farm. From there we ventured to the tomato patch. I hoped to impress them with the amazing sweet flavor of my golden, cherry tomatoes, the only cherries I was willing to grow, for they are very labor intensive to pick. My 'Sungold' tomatoes were at the end of their harvest. The vines were droopy and tired—not exactly horticultural specimens to proudly show off. We were no longer picking them for customers, but there were still glistening, golden orbs to be found among the defoliating vines, inviting onlookers to sample. "You're welcome to try some," I told the group. One girl was bolder than her parent and accepted the invitation. Her small hands gently grasped a cherry tomato and slowly raised it to her mouth. It popped between her teeth. Her eyes opened wide to the surprise of a sweet, ripe cherry tomato bursting its flavor onto her taste buds. She grabbed another and another. The parents and other children spread out over the patch, searching for their own experience, eagerly plucking tomatoes from the vines. Each found the round treasures to indeed be a special taste treat, something they would remember far longer than anything I had said in the farm stand.

One father in the group would later tell Danielle that cherry tomatoes were now his daughter's preferred snack at home. It was a small revelation, but one that Danielle knew could have a positive, life-changing effect on her students and their children. These eye-opening farm visits were the experiences she was hoping to share with her students. She was planting seeds in her own way.

Any experience that helps us take a second look at what we eat works to make a connection to our food. It brings mindfulness to the journey—the soil, sunshine, and care—it has taken to land on our plates. These experiences nudge us to question why all tomatoes don't taste as good as those 'Sungold'. And if we pursue that inquiry, we learn that someone else has been making decisions for us about our food choices. It's easy to abdicate responsibility for our food in the name of speed and convenience. But even when we do choose to cook at home, producing healthy, good-tasting meals can be a challenge. Out-of-season tomatoes sold in many grocery stores—what I call "cardboard" tomatoes—are bred so that they can be shipped without harm, without much concern for flavor or nutritional value. These tomatoes also are shipped unripe, without the opportunity to develop vine-ripened flavor or nutrients. In contrast, a delicate, tasty vine-ripened tomato does not stand up to abuse. Shipping them can result in the arrival of tomato sauce at their destination. If you can't visit a farm like Danielle's class did, your backyard garden, local farm stand, or nearby farmer's market are the best places to find perfectly ripened tomatoes.

Simply put, we take our food for granted. Just like the water that comes through our tap from some unseen source, our grocery stores bulge with edibles disconnected from their origins. There are many things that we're disconnected from in our lives. We pump gas without remembering the journey it has taken from the depths of Earth, to a refinery, across an ocean or a continent. Sidewalks keep us separate from the Earth's crust. It is remarkable that we can live in cocoons all our lives without even touching the soil that nurtures the food we eat. But can a shrink-wrapped life really sustain us? Ask any child who, given the choice between the shaved nubbin of an unmarketable "baby carrot," reduced of its nutritionally rich skin and found in a plastic bag in the grocery store, and a carrot that they've planted and pulled from the garden by its green, frilly leaves and stems, washed and eaten on the spot—ask that child which is more full of life-giving force. Unless he or she has been taught to fear dirt and the out-of-doors, it's no contest. And once that connection is made, there's no going back. They've discovered the sacred.

The following spring, Danielle returned with a new crop of students. They gingerly stepped among the strawberry plants, leaned over awkwardly, and pulled aside leaves to search for red treasures. One young woman wore flip flops—not appropriate for farm fields, even those with carpets of straw between the rows of berries. She screamed and frantically swatted the air as insects flew by.

Another young woman popped a strawberry into her mouth. "These are really good, Danielle," she said.

"They're not what you may be used to from the grocery store," Danielle replied. I handed out the pint berry boxes to the students that wanted them. There was no going back to the hard, flavorless berries in the grocery stores. What a dilemma! Enlightenment can be uncomfortable. It made one wonder what else they had been missing.

My experience with learning what good food tastes like began like so many others—growing up on a farm with a large garden. It was what helped sustain a large family when money was tight. My father planted our gardens in the red, sandy soils of eastern Oklahoma with potatoes, corn, green beans, summer squashes, cucumbers, tomatoes, okra, and cowpeas. When I began my farming venture, I lived in the black soils of Iowa and a northern climate. It was much easier to grow the cool-weather crops that didn't do as well in Oklahoma—spinach and broccoli—and much harder to grow the heat-loving cowpeas.

The growing, cooking, and preserving of food was and is a tradition passed on by our ancestors, although not so much anymore. An entire generation has forgotten or not been taught how to do this. The ease and convenience of finding prepared food at restaurants and grocery stores has grown immensely during my lifetime. People now earn money to buy the very things they no longer have the time or the inclination to do in their lives, whether it's growing and cooking their food or repairing and painting their home. This brings a disconnect to the world around them. Countless times my customers and even employees were surprised to see how asparagus stalks arise from the ground in the spring, bare and leafless. They don't know which vegetables or fruits can be frozen or dried for future use. The fact that some crops such as beets can be stored in the refrigerator for months and lettuce won't last two weeks is a mystery to them.

When Danielle's student had frantically swatted at flying insects, it brought to mind where I learned patience with the tiny creatures in my youth. On the farm, the air around Mother and me would buzz with wasps in their yellow and black striped coats. We were nervous to work around them, but they had no thoughts of harming us. What could we expect? They were hungry and thirsty on those hot, dry Oklahoma summer days, and we were standing in a patch of 'Purple hull' cowpeas, their sweet, perfumed blossoms of nectar beckoning. Resisting any urge to swat or even accidentally come in contact with the insects, we silently continued our picking of the peas into the large baskets we toted along with us. The reddish-purple peas hovered on stems at the top of the plants like pencils bulging with the peas inside.

As our baskets slowly filled, I dreamed about a better way to spend my summer days that would include work for pay like some of my friends who had jobs in town. My brothers did not help with the garden harvest. They were off hauling hay for summer jobs. But I couldn't complain too loudly as they had chores that I didn't have to participate in, like milking our cow twice a day or repairing fences.

Mother and I eventually carried our full baskets into the house and sat in front of droning fans and the afternoon TV game shows to make our time shelling the peas a little less onerous on a hot day. These peas would then be blanched and put in the freezer along with corn and green beans and the meat from our farm animals. And when they were brought out for a winter meal, I was much more appreciative of their hearty flavor and the work we had put in. The connection I had to this vegetable's journey to our plates gave it new respect and meaning.

Growing food for any CSA involves a wide variety of crops so there are vegetables to fill the box every week for the entire summer. In my case, I felt like a child in a candy store as I selected seeds from the garden catalogs each winter. Who knew there were so many shapes, colors, and sizes of eggplant? What planet did kohlrabi or 'Romanesco' broccoli come from? And who named these vegetables—'Mortgage Lifter' tomato, 'Bodacious' sweet corn, 'Hinkelhatz' peppers, 'Triamble' winter squash? I loved it all. But for my consumers, new tastes and visual sensations could be overwhelming and confusing. They sometimes felt way out of their comfort zone. Some could not even recognize the produce. I felt it was my job to help them connect with the positive attributes of these new vegetables.

Once I received an email from one of my customers asking "What's this spiny, round, yellowish vegetable in our box this week?" My customers were notorious for not reading the newsletter that accompanied their weekly share.

"That would be a 'Lemon' cucumber," I wrote back. "Pretty obvious how it got its name, don't you think?" My customer had described this heirloom vegetable perfectly, illustrating how vegetables sometimes come in shapes or colors different from what we are used to. Harder questions came about greens—kale, arugula, mustard greens, broccoli rabe, spinach, lettuce, or bok choy. The great variety could also be puzzling, even when the name of a vegetable hints strongly about its character.

"Is this lettuce diseased?" someone wanted to know about her 'Freckles' lettuce.

"No," I reassured her. "It's supposed to have those spots." 'Freckles' is a beautiful bright green, romaine lettuce with crimson speckles. It originated in Austria where it was called 'Forellenschluss' or 'Speckled Trout'.

We harvested most vegetables the same day of delivery, and customers were amazed at how long the produce stayed fresh in their refrigerators. "I can't believe how nice my spinach is a week later in my refrigerator," one woman said. I left unspoken my concern that she still hadn't eaten that vegetable a week later. I used the opportunity to explain about how long grocery store produce might have been on the shelf or in transit before even being purchased.

But freshness is not always a recognized characteristic. A farm colleague, Virginia Moser, once told me about an encounter with one of her customers at a farmer's market. The woman was someone who Virginia remembered had purchased items from her the previous week. "I think there was something wrong with the eggs that you sold me last week, so I threw them out," the woman complained. "The whites of the eggs stayed under the yolk like a thick, firm, gelatinous mass instead of spreading out into the pan like usual."

Virginia was surprised and dismayed by the woman's actions but spoke up to educate her. "That's the sign of a fresh egg. The ones with a flat, runny white have been around a while." Once again, those connections to and knowledge about what the freshest food looks and tastes like remain absent from many of our daily lives.

The taste and visual appeal of our food can lead to changes in our food choices. That focus can lead us to appreciate our food. The planting, tending, and nurturing of the plant that produces that food or the care of the animal that becomes our food greatly deepens that connection and experience. I glory in the wonder of my backyard chickens just being chickens from the day they were hatched. Seeing a green line of an emerging row of spinach or radishes breaking through the soil surface still strikes awe in me that all this can come from a tiny seed. It knows how to grow on its own. I just need to get out of the way. Farming can be like parenthood. Nurture and guide, allow and protect, respect and love. Namaste, if you will—the God in me recognizing the God in them, whether it's our children or our food.

My farming colleagues and I likely had those feelings about the sacred in food and farming almost simultaneously, and that's what brought us together. I attribute those feelings to a reaction to the increasing environmental concerns of how food was being grown. In the wider world, oil spills, nuclear accidents (Three Mile Island), and chemical pollution (Love Canal) were damaging soils and water, creating unhealthy living conditions, and resulting in acid rain in the 1970s. In agriculture across the Upper Midwest, increased use of pesticides and fertilizers was contaminating the air and waterways. The farm crisis of the 1980s saw the consolidation of farms as many farmers went out of business. This increased the size of farms and a movement toward intensive monocropping for efficiency. Agriculture was becoming an industry that seemed more interested in high yields without regard to the costs to soil, air, water, and sustainability.

Those feelings led us to want to farm in partnership with Earth and all its living things as best we could. Learning about CSAs helped us seek out the support of our customers for what we were doing. There were people like

Danielle who were not farmers but still valued the importance of how food was produced. We were eager to help
pioneer this new (yet old) way of farming in our local communities. Luckily there were many more who were willing
to support the CSA ventures.

Those in the local food scene in Iowa in the late 1990s
were encouraged even further by Drake University agriculture law professor Neil Hamilton, who had been attending
and speaking at sustainable farming conferences. Neil was
short in stature with boyish good looks and the utmost
politeness. He talked in a measured, intellectual manner
and looked at both sides of an argument as any good lawyer would. And he could cut to the chase to make a point.
His interest in food and agriculture stemmed from his
own farm where he and his wife grew vegetables for local
restaurants. In speaking to farmers at conference dinners,
he challenged them, "Look at your plate. How much of this
food did you grow or produce? Why are you not eating
your own food at these dinners? Here in Iowa we boast
that we are the breadbasket of the world, yet we import 80
percent of our food. Valuing our work and our food begins
with ourselves."

At our meetings my farming colleagues and I began to
honor the food we had brought for a potluck or for other
local dinners with reverence and pride. Placards with the
contributions of local farms were placed on each table to
be read by the diners. We recognized these farmers at the
meals so that everyone knew the face behind the food.
At gatherings where the food was provided by a facility,
we approached the kitchen staff and worked with them
to find local sources for menu items. I was amazed when
I attended a conference in Wisconsin around this time
where everything in the meal was locally sourced except

for the salt and chocolate. We applauded the chefs at these dinners for their contributions before the eating began. Grace wasn't said, but it was implicit. We were honoring our food and, by so doing, honoring each other, our bodies, the Earth, and other living beings.

I feel that food assimilation could be more intimate and important than sex. Three times a day or more we have a date with food. We ingest substances that our bodies assimilate into our core, our being. We expose ourselves to their life-altering influences. We become one with our food. How could we treat this sacred ritual like a one-night stand with strange foods in a box from the grocery aisle or a frivolous fling with a fast-food restaurant menu? We are a nation of riches, and we have more food choices than at any other time in our history. But what do wise choices look and taste like? When I started my CSA, I wanted to be a part of providing my community with wise, healthy choices.

As nature writer and agrarian activist Gary Paul Nabhan asks in *Coming Home to Eat,* "Just what exactly is it that we want to have cross our lips, to roll off our tongues, down our throats, to fill our nostrils with hardly described fragrances, to slide to a brief halt within our bellies . . . and then to be lodged within our very own bodies? What do we want to be made of? What do we claim as our tastes? And what on earth do we ultimately want to taste like?"

We can wisely choose who grows our food, how it is grown, and how we prepare that food. But it takes time, it takes effort, it takes mindfulness. CSA customers make an intentional choice to be a part of a farm. But they are doing more than simply placating their hunger pangs with fuel to get to the next meal. They appreciate the substance and the experience of life, the care of the soil and water that showed up along with their CSA boxes.

At the end of their spring visit, I led Danielle's students to the asparagus patch and asked them if they would like to try some. I snapped off several spears arising from the row of ferny plants.

"I've heard raw asparagus is poisonous," a young woman suggested.

"Well, if that were true, I'd be dead," I surmised. "The farm crew nibbles on spears as we harvest, and I can assure you we're all happy and healthy."

One brave volunteer raised her hands to try the delicacy. She tentatively put the tip of the spear between her teeth. As she chewed the small bite, she smiled and gave a small nod of approval. This wasn't as popular a treat as the strawberries or cherry tomatoes had been, but perhaps it was just as enlightening an experience for the students. They would remember the intricacies of this vegetable. They would remember the different flavors and a new way to eat asparagus. And, perhaps more importantly, we were planting those seeds of hope that Danielle wished for, having them savor all the sacred wonder and connection that this food and all food had to offer.

4

THE SUPPORT NETWORK

Call it a clan, call it a network, call it a tribe, call it
a family. Whatever you call it, whoever you are, you
need one.

—KATHERINE MACKENZIE-SMITH

THE MASTER OF HORTICULTURE DEGREE that I pursued
from 1992 to 1995 was giving me good basic plant knowledge, but there was only one class in sustainable horticulture offered in my program. Sustainable agriculture or
horticulture tries to meet society's food and textile needs
in the present without compromising the ability of future
generations to meet their needs. A healthy environment
is important, but profitability and social and economic
equity are, too. My desire to learn about organic farming was not being met in the classroom. I didn't feel like I
could just jump into the field and start farming with book
knowledge alone. I wanted to wrap my brain around the
nuts and bolts of working in the physical environment,
nurturing the plants and animals, and doing my best to
take care of the living soil. I was impatient. To fill some of
that void, I explored extracurricular activities at conferences and meetings with like-minded people.

I put a cassette in the player in my car and started my
forty-five minute journey to Ames, Iowa. As a graduate

student commuter to school at Iowa State University (ISU), I had little time for recreational listening. These drives between home and school were a welcome escape from the books. I'd just received a set of tapes from the Upper Midwest Organic Farming Conference in Sinsinawa Mound, Wisconsin, a four-hour drive away. I hadn't been able to attend it with my school schedule this particular year although I would in future years. The session recordings were a wonderful way for those of us who could not attend to gather strands of shared knowledge from those who could and were sharing it. On one tape, a farmer recorded ways to encourage beneficial insects on his farm. Another talked about weed control. This networking with other farmers was one of the most beneficial and practical ways to learn about farming.

The first cassette tape was on a topic of great interest to me: community-supported agriculture, or CSA, an idea built on cooperation instead of competition. Eaters joined forces with growers to work together to get food on the plate. Today, community-supported agriculture is anything but novel, but in the 1990s it brought me a lightning bolt of inspiration. Enlightened people who cared about how their food was grown were taking proactive steps to support the farmers of their choice who also loved and cared for the soil, the plants, and animals. It seemed like a win-win relationship to me. I could spend less time marketing my crops if I already had dedicated customers lined up. There was no question that these vegetables and fruits would have a home to welcome them. I could gauge the amount of produce to grow for these loyal customers. Food that was picked and delivered the same day couldn't get any fresher.

CSAs educate their customers about a wide variety of vegetables that they might have shied away from in the past. They also provide a bigger market for some vegetables that wouldn't have been top picks from a farm stand. When I began farming, I would place things like kohlrabi, turnips, and cooking greens in the CSA box—not the usual menu items in the 1990s—until they became familiar to my customers along with the more common (and sometimes far less interesting) vegetables like corn, green beans, and tomatoes. I can still remember watching Linda Halley, at that time with Harmony Valley Farm in Wisconsin, at a workshop during the Upper Midwest Organic Farming Conference as she showed the contents of a fall box from her farm. When a stalk of Brussels sprouts appeared with the sprouts still attached, my mouth gaped open. Not only was she providing the vegetable in a show-stopping manner, she was educating the CSA members about how the food actually grew.

This community support for farmers was a financial partnership as well. It came with an abundance of trust for the promise of a future harvest. Members paid up front for their season of vegetables, sharing the costs of supporting the farm, including the risks. Expenses for the farmer start each year in January with seed purchases, labor, and equipment needs, even though the produce won't appear for months. In turn, members received local, fresh, wholesome food grown sustainably and responsibly by a farmer they knew. It was really quite simple! The produce hadn't traveled across the continent and was generally harvested the same day of delivery. Most CSAs promote biodiversity, education, and the role of agriculture in the community. It helps to assure the continued existence of the local producer of these food products by allowing the farmer to receive the whole food dollar. Word-of-mouth recommendations were another source for networking that came from people I met on campus. This led me to off-campus resources that went beyond the classroom.

My horticulture advisor Gail Nonnecke encouraged me to talk with Shelley Gradwell, a like-minded student in the agronomy department. Shelley worked for Ricardo Salvador, an ISU professor who went on to become a senior scientist and director of the Food & Environment Program for the Union of Concerned Scientists. She was tall and thin with long, straight blond hair and freckles. She looked like she could still be in high school. From the beginning Shelley was enthusiastic about all things relating to local food and sustainable agriculture. "There are people here in Ames who are starting a CSA," she told me. "Usually farmers start the CSAs, but a group of us who aren't current farmers, but want to have access to fresh, healthy food, are trying to get this going. We're calling it Magic Beanstalk," she said, before inviting me to a potluck gathering to learn more. I was surprised to be presented with activities like this while still in graduate school, but I was anxious to put my finger on the pulse of what was happening in Iowa.

Magic Beanstalk was a CSA with multiple producers contributing to the share. It was initiated in 1995 with the help of the Kellogg Foundation–funded Shared Visions program. This CSA's purpose was to make locally grown food and fiber products available to residents in the Ames, Iowa area. It later expanded with the Field to Family Project that focused on nutritional education, seasonal meals, and farm activities for children and families; help for low-income people to get access to fresh fruits and vegetables; and building partnerships with churches, social service groups, and educational organizations. They hoped these activities would foster an understanding of and appreciation for sustainable agriculture.

Learning about Magic Beanstalk began the unfolding process of meeting others also interested in this concept of CSAs and local food in Iowa. Through this meeting and many more I came into contact with others who had had similar inspiration to pursue this topic and vocation. None of them were current students. We began to gather and network. We were green, but hungry for information. Most of us had not grown food for markets, but only within the bounds of our backyard gardens. But this was about more than just producing vegetables. It was about growing healthy food and finding community around that food.

CSAs were nonexistent in Iowa in the early 1990s. Some of our education about them took us outside the state. Minnesota and Wisconsin were ahead of the game in the Upper Midwest, although, as with many things, the coasts were where the ideas had first taken hold in the United States. Worldwide beginnings of CSAs appear to have first started in Japan in 1965 as "teikei" (food with the farmer's face on it) farms. Consumers promised local farmers direct sales in exchange for healthier methods of production—fewer pesticides, fewer processed and imported foods. This idea of a direct, committed relationship between consumers and producers of food spread to Europe and then the United States.

Trauger Groh of Temple-Wilton Community Farm, a biodynamic farm in New Hampshire, and Robyn Van En of Indian Line Farm CSA in Massachusetts (and later with Jon Vandertuin at Brookline Community Farm) started the first CSAs in the United States in 1986. Groh had come over from similar farms in Germany, and Vandertuin had worked on farms in Switzerland and brought this exciting idea to Van En. Groh and Van En both promoted this type of agriculture by writing books, speaking at conferences, and hosting visitors at their farms. CSAs were an idea with merit that was being seized upon quickly by the farming community. Others had felt resonance for this model years earlier, just as I had now.

It only took two more years for the first CSA to start in the Upper Midwest. Educators Peter and Bernadette Seeley met at the Scattergood Quaker School in Iowa. Peter was from New England and taught math. Bernadette came from the Netherlands and taught physical education. Neither had previous farming backgrounds, but Scattergood, which had a farm as part of its educational program, gave them inspiration. In the fall of 1986 they traveled to New England to visit some farms. Someone suggested they visit Trauger Groh's farm where they learned about his CSA concept. They found the idea appealing and decided to visit more CSA farms in the Northeast. One of these was Robyn Van En's Indian Line Farm. After those visits to the East, Peter and Bernadette worked a year in Missouri at a market garden to gain experience. They moved to Wisconsin and started Springdale Community Farm in 1988.

My first visit to a CSA farm was Common Harvest in Minnesota near Minneapolis in the fall of 1995. Dan Guenthner and his wife Margaret Pinnings had begun farming there in 1990 on rented ground (where I visited) until they later landed in Osceola, Wisconsin, for a permanent location. I saw equipment for vegetable crops that I had never seen—tine weeders, basket weeders, wheel hoes. His fall crops of greens and root crops still in the field and a shed full of winter squashes opened my eyes to possibilities of season extension and fed my enthusiasm. That same fall I visited the Philadelphia Community Farm in Osceola, which further expanded my awareness of the different kinds of CSAs people were creating. Philadelphia was a biodynamic farm with educational opportunities for the community. Rudolf Steiner, a philosopher and scientist, inspired this type of farming in the 1920s as a way to combine the science of agriculture with the spirit of the land. Biodynamic farms use not only organic principles, but additional production methods to integrate and harmonize the soil, compost, farm animals, crops, forests, people, and the spirit of the place as a whole living organism. I appreciated this concept but felt overextended to incorporate these more complex practices when I was a beginning farmer without animals on my farm.

Our loose band of potential farmers in Iowa decided we could learn from a visit to our northern neighbors in Minnesota as a group. Some of us made plans to visit several CSAs near Northfield. We were from diverse places, ages, and experiences, but with unbounded enthusiasm for a system of farming that met our values. Jeff Hall was a young librarian in Ames with visions of his own farm but did not yet own land. Jan Libby, who would be farming with her husband, Tim Landgraf, even before he quit his mechanical engineering job, lived on a farm in northern Iowa. Gary Guthrie and his wife Nancy had spent several years in Bolivia and El Salvador living and working with the *campesinos* as Mennonite volunteers and were returning to his family farm near Ames. Virginia Moser was along hoping to get ideas for her and her husband's vegetable farm in eastern Iowa. I was farming on rented ground at this point. We were each piecing together how this new idea of farming might work for us. We bounced ideas off each other for reality checks to temper our excitement.

I stopped my van precariously halfway up the long hill of a snow-covered road in rural Minnesota near the driveway, covered in six inches of snow, of the CSA farmers we were scheduled to meet. My van was no four-wheel drive vehicle. I knew as soon as I stopped I could not continue uphill. My occupants got out of the van, pulling up their parkas and scarves to meet the chill of the winter air. I was able to turn the vehicle around, go down the hill, and come back with enough speed to make it to the top of the hill.

Sharing this van was one way I could help this fledgling group of beginning farmers. Even though it was a gas guzzler, it used less gas than if we all had driven separately. I found a place to park and then walked halfway down the hill to join the group that was waiting patiently. We trudged down the driveway of the farmhouse for our planned visit. Sitting in a warm, sunlit room in the farmhouse, we picked the brains of the owner and several other local farmers on how this whole CSA movement was working for them. Each of them ran their CSAs differently. One of them was a teacher and only operated during the summer months when school was out. Another did not live on his farm. Some did deliveries, others used drop sites. Not all their crops were alike. We all had circumstances that would make our CSAs different from each other, too. Virginia would have egg shares, Jan would sell chicken meat shares, Gary's specialty became carrots and mine strawberries. This was just the information we were looking for. Nothing else could have gotten me onto that treacherous road in the middle of a Minnesota winter.

Our next stop was further north in an area near St. Paul with acreages on the edge of the city. David Washburn, co-owner of Red Cardinal Farm with his wife Meg Anderson, had agreed to speak with us. When we arrived, he jumped into the van with us on this cold, winter day while we quizzed him relentlessly. We got a tour of his garden— at least as much as one can see with a foot of snow on the ground. Beautiful three-foot-high lacinato kale plants still held their harvestable leaves drooping down at the sides, but most of the other produce were just cellulosic skeletons of their former selves slowly being reclaimed by the earth. His equipment storage shed could have housed several tennis courts, and he had machinery that was way beyond our beginners' group of wannabe veggie growers' dreams.

Perhaps the most important thing that he shared with us was that he was reevaluating whether he would continue this business. He was a former businessman and was good at seeing the economic realities of this venture. He and his wife wanted to have children and didn't want to live in poverty. Years later, we'd learn that these trailblazers did follow through on their decision to leave active farming, although they continued to mentor beginning farmers and rented them their farm ground. Small-scale farming is not a lucrative business. That is why the majority of farmers have off-farm jobs to help support their passion in a society that places high value on certain crops. There are government subsidies for corn and soybeans, but not for vegetables and fruits. This can make small farms a riskier economic venture (although many corn and soybean farmers or their spouses work off-farm, too).

There are obvious costs for any family to consider along with the economics of a farming career. Each person has their own interests to follow, their own sorting of priorities. Gary Guthrie's response to people who asked him if he could make a living farming was to reframe it and say he knew he could make a life. I couldn't imagine starting a farm while having children to raise and a spouse who was fully employed in another field. My children were in college and high school when I went to graduate school. By the time I started farming in 1996, they were self-sufficient young women. Amy, the eldest, worked for me part-time my first farming summer before she moved to Colorado. I can remember her screams when she encountered spiders, her least favorite creature. Kristin, the youngest, had too many pollen allergies to spend that much time in the outdoors. I had the emotional support of my husband and our children—it just wasn't in the field.

That creative ball of inspiration burning in the occupants of that van in Minnesota along with others similarly inspired back in Iowa set things into motion. By January of 1996, we created a new organization called Iowa Network for Community Agriculture (INCA) from a Sustainable Agriculture Research and Education (SARE) Program grant. I served briefly as secretary and joined educational efforts to mentor others. With an evangelical fervor, we began holding our own Iowa conferences, teaching others about CSAs and farming techniques, about the small equipment needs and methods of production. We invited Dan Guenthner to give the keynote address at our first conference in October 1996. Jay Robinson, a librarian turned minister who was anxious to promote local food with his congregation, volunteered his church in northern Iowa to host the event. We shared stories of what worked and what didn't, where we could find land, how to meet sustainable or organic standards, how to manage a CSA. We met people statewide that seemed to have that light bulb moment and a desire for the same kind of information at the same time. INCA eventually widened its focus to include marketing and information about local food systems to address the growing interest in this topic.

It wasn't long after we formed INCA that Shelly Gradwell continued her nudges. "Angela, you should attend a

Practical Farmers of Iowa (PFI) meeting. They're another grassroots organization that you might like."

I wasn't looking for another organization to take time out of my life. My farm was already becoming all consuming. I had trouble even calling myself a "farmer" since vegetable farming was more commonly labeled "market gardening." There was no instant kinship or desire to explore it further. Weren't these row-crop and animal farmers that I had little in common with? What could I learn about vegetable and fruit production from them? Besides, what's a "practical" farmer? Graduate school was behind me, and organizing my CSA felt like a full plate. I felt no need to stick my toe into a wider circle of agriculture. But I also realized I still had much to learn. I appeased Shelly by replying, "Tell me more about it and why I should go."

"Well, some innovative Iowa farmers started it," she explained. "The farm crisis of the eighties made them want to find more efficient ways to reduce expensive inputs, and diversified farms seemed to be a key, you know, keeping the animals and crops together on the farms. They do on-farm research that's inspired by farmers rather than professors," she replied. "Then they have field days to share what they've learned with other farmers."

PFI was started about ten years prior to INCA. Dick and Sharon Thompson and Larry Kallem initiated the organization. It was the parallel group to INCA's vegetable and small animal farmers for sustainable row-crop and diversified farm operations. I could appreciate the value of farmer networking after our Minnesota visit and some of the conferences that I had attended or listened to on tapes. There were other organizations in Minnesota and Wisconsin that were instrumental in helping sustainable farms. The Land Stewardship Project was formed in 1982 and initially organized

"Soil Stewardship Ethics" meetings in Minnesota, Iowa, and the Dakotas to create changes in the food and farming systems that promote stewardship, justice, and democracy. In Wisconsin, an organization named Madison Area Community Supported Agriculture Coalition (MACSAC), formed in 1992 by supporters and wannabe farmers, aimed to find cooperative development for local CSA farmers. Other helpful organizations or programs included Appropriate Technology Transfer for Rural Areas (ATTRA), SARE, and university extension services. The farm crisis of the 1980s likely contributed to the formation of all these organizations. Overproduction of grain crops and subsequent low prices, the consolidation of farms due to bankruptcy, and the presence of smaller affordable farms all changed the picture of agriculture in the Upper Midwest around this time. All farmers were looking for a way to survive.

The winter after my first year farming, I attended a PFI gathering. My vegetable farming colleagues also began attending meetings, so it became a valuable opportunity to network with them. Introverted and reluctant though I was, I recognized that I was finding real value in learning what I didn't know from far more experienced farmers. The Cooperators' Meetings that PFI held in February discussed farmers' ideas for on-farm research that would benefit their operations. Several of these ideas would be chosen by the farmers, and two or three volunteered to do the research. Rick Exner, an early organizer and employee of PFI, started one small group session there that I attended. "Everyone introduce yourself and where you farm," he requested. I was near the front and spoke up in turn.

"Angela Tedesco, Turtle Farm at Granger, Iowa. I grow organic fruits and vegetables for a CSA," I said.

There was only one other woman seated among about

thirty men. As the introductions continued down the rows of seated participants and got to her, she remained silent and her husband spoke for them both. I was flabbergasted. I wanted to speak up and say, "Wait, what's your name? You're important, too," but since this was my first meeting, I held my tongue. There were no other horticulture farmers present in the room, so I felt like an anomaly. No one in the group spoke to me after the session.

Afterwards I approached Rick, whom I had met on several previous occasions, and said, "I think everyone, even the women, should introduce themselves and not be ignored." I wondered how I would fit in with this group of male-dominated, row-crop farmers even if they were diversified. Crops of corn and soybeans grown primarily for animal feed were not my area. I was interested in feeding people directly. The CSA farmers were more equally represented between men and women. Continuing with this organization would be an adjustment.

Rick seemed cognizant that there could be improvement, and I believe he acted on it in the future. Certainly two of PFI's cofounders, Dick and Sharon Thompson, often acted as a duo in their research presentations. This was refreshing. They frequently spoke of their divine inspiration to change their methods from straight conventional farming, which Dick had eagerly embraced after getting his degree in agriculture at ISU, back to the more sustainable farming that his father had used when he was growing up. Conventional farming found them wanting more answers. They kept detailed records, used statistical analysis, and always used farmer-initiated questions to direct their research. Dick often shared their insights, including what kept them going as the mavericks in their farming community—"get along, but don't go along."

I didn't attend too many row-crop conference sessions or field days since my focus was horticulture, but when I did, I surprisingly often found useful ideas that could apply to both farming types such as improving our soils with cover crops that got tilled in, dealing with pests, or passing on the farm to others. One of the most helpful ideas that I gleaned from Dick and Sharon Thompson that could apply to horticulture was the idea of weeding bare fields or "stale beds."

Dick, tall and slender with a farmer's tan and graying hair, began a weed control workshop in his usual slow, precise, and thoughtful recitation. "This method of weed control requires some patience, which is not always found in farmers that are anxious to get their crops in the ground in the spring. It does lead to good results though, at least with annual weeds. After the first tillage of the season, the farmer holds off on planting immediately. Instead the field remains fallow for a week or so, giving weeds a chance to barely sprout. Rainfall is helpful here." Dick was good at pointing out practicalities. He continued to explain that a second, shallow tillage is done to remove those tiny emerging weeds. The crops can then be planted, or the process can be repeated a second time. The initial deeper tillage turns up many weed seeds that need light for germination. The following shallow tillage disrupts those in the zone where light can reach them and does not turn up many more that have not already germinated. "Of course the success of this method is dependent upon the weather cooperating—like everything else in farming," he said, ending his talk. The method was one I began to use every time the weather would allow. One good idea like this made any conference or meeting worth its price of admission.

Eventually most of INCA's producer members grav-
itated to PFI, and the community showed us grace and
acceptance. That was not always found in other groups.
I had been to horticulture meetings where the farmers
wouldn't share their ideas out of a sense of competition. I
had also attended a traditional farmers' group where I had
been challenged by a man who indignantly questioned,
"You call what you do farming?" I was taken aback by his
comment. I didn't know this person. I assumed he was a
row-crop farmer who thought size of farm and amount
of equipment made a person a farmer. Small farms are
sometimes thought of as "hobby farms" by those who do
not realize that horticultural crops can produce thousands
of times the value per acre of a row crop. Another time, in
a group of women landowners convened by the Women,
Food and Agriculture Network (WFAN), a traditional
farmer had spoken before I was to speak. When it came
my turn, he sarcastically interjected, "I suppose you want
to feed the world."

I replied, "No, I hope to just feed a small part of Iowa." I
could have added that Iowa imports 80 percent of its food
despite having some of the most fertile and productive land
in the world. That was not always the case. In the 1920s there
were fifty-eight canneries for the vegetable crops grown
in Iowa, and it was the country's sixth largest producer of
grapes. I could have told him that at one time it was one of
the top apple growing states, but the devastating Armistice
Day freeze of 1940 decimated the apple production and
growers never recovered. He may have known that with
increased subsidies for corn and soybeans, it became easier and more desirable to grow row crops, while crops like
grapes were incompatible with the chemicals and sprays
being used on corn and soybeans.

I couldn't determine if these affronts were because of my gender, because I practiced sustainable agriculture, or maybe these farmers just didn't like vegetables. Occurrences like this are one reason that WFAN would often have such discussions without men present because it changed the dynamics in the room. Women landowners may have been bullied by their renters or felt incompetent to stand up for their own land-management decisions. They learned and shared better with other women. I had experienced many times when my husband John was present that men would direct farming questions to him rather than me. I loved his response once in such an encounter when he said, "I can barely put gas in the car. If you have a farming question you better ask her."

Like INCA, PFI became like family. They were as eager for information as we were. Our merging ideas sparked creativity and broadened horizons in both groups. After all, we were both on the same page of sustainable agriculture. Both organizations used farmer networking and programing ideas. Both shared the same values of building healthy soils, healthy food, and vibrant communities. Nothing spoke to that more than PFI's 2002 Annual Report:

It's so obvious, so provocative, but so curious: why are we the practical farmers of Iowa? Why not the innovative, or sustainable, or holistic farmers of Iowa? Or as was recently proposed: the romantic farmers of Iowa. And who has not been asked: is there such a thing as an impractical farmer of Iowa?

Consider: A farming system that requires a tractor so large and complicated a farmer can't fix it, a globalized food system that doesn't benefit farmers, a state that feeds the world but not itself.

Perhaps they are the greatest dangers of our time:

vision without practicality—efficiency without common sense.

Imagine drawing on the wisdom of farmers and the needs of the land when we: design farming systems, create new food supply chains, consider new farm policies. Perhaps being practical means: remembering the land when we are in the laboratory, remembering the consumer when we are in the field, remembering the farmer when we are in the grocery store.

Eventually PFI programming would expand even further beyond horticulture to topics of diversification including animal grazing, cover crops, soil health, and beginning farmer support. For many people in Iowa and beyond, myself included, the organization continues to be their go-to farming resource. For sixteen years I relied on the support of PFI for on-farm research. The goal of PFI on-farm research was to address issues important to the farmer. Why not put that irritating or chronic problem on the farm to a test to find improvement? That was a bottom-up approach rather than top-down from academic institutions or commercial interests that searched for a farm willing to demonstrate their research. Sometimes the interests of the farmer and academics meshed and served both their interests. University professors or other researchers would often attend the PFI Cooperators' Meeting to find common ground for this work. A few other organizations (SARE, Organic Farming Research Foundation, and Pennsylvania Association for Sustainable Agriculture) began funding farmer-generated ideas using competitive grants.

With PFI's support, in 2009 Gail Nonnecke and I searched for a better method of weed control in the pathways between raspberry plantings, a particular concern among organic farmers. We knew that tillage, which was often used to reduce weed growth, often left the soil vulnerable to erosion and could deplete nutrients and organic matter from the topsoil. As an alternative, we tried growing a living mulch of turfgrass, dwarf white clover, bird's-foot trefoil, or alfalfa on the soil surface. The latter three are members of the legume family Fabaceae and provide nitrogen to the soil. The clover proved far more effective than the other treatments and reduced both the germination of new weed seeds and the need for tilling. An unexpected result that was not documented in our research was that the increased fertility from the legume cover crops actually increased the production of the raspberries.

Other ISU professors helped me with insect control research in strawberries and cucurbits (melons, pumpkin, squash, and cucumbers), often in conjunction with PFI or the Leopold Center, but sometimes directly. The Leopold Center for Sustainable Agriculture at ISU was created through the 1987 Iowa Groundwater Protection Act by the Iowa legislature and named for Aldo Leopold, the conservationist, ecologist, and educator. My master's research with Gail Nonnecke was the first horticulture grant made possible by the center whose mission facilitates sustainable agriculture research and education.

Farming from books or lectures in a classroom or even from the plans we put on paper was sterile. Getting into the field and facing the complicated intersections of soil life, soil types, pests, weather, and the labor and equipment to do it all was like a giant puzzle. Every season gave me a new challenge. Advice from other farmers—a real support network—turned out to be one of the best ways to find those missing pieces from the puzzle.

5

CSA STARTS
WITH COMMUNITY

There is no power for change greater than a community
discovering what it cares about.
—MARGARET J. WHEATLEY

AFTER I HAD BEEN FARMING for several years, Gail Nonnecke invited me to speak to her Sustainable Horticulture
classes about community-supported agriculture (CSA).
Once we got past the "do you know where your food comes
from" discussions, one of the points I always emphasized
was the importance of relationships and cooperation in
this model of agriculture. I would illustrate this by drawing a simple triangle on the board. "This is my personal
symbol for community-supported agriculture," I would
say. "Each side of the triangle represents one aspect. The
first is the farming community—that's me and my farm
workers. The second side represents the consumer community—my customers. The third side is the foundation
to it all, the Earth community—all the living entities in
and on the land. If any one side is absent, the triangle col-
lapses: they're all important."

People don't have trouble imagining farmers and customers as communities, but many of us haven't thought

of life beyond the human species on (or in) the Earth as a community. Working farms are teeming with life that decomposes organic matter and makes nutrients available to sustain plants and other life within the soil. The soil is literally a food web. Bacteria, protozoa, earthworms, centipedes, fungi, nematodes, slugs, insects, spiders, and small rodents live in the soil profile and provide food for each other. They also provide food for plants, birds, and mammals on the surface. These living organisms improve soil structure and its ability to absorb rainfall. Caring for the soil and, ultimately, the food it produces is the best way to nurture this complex community. It was a responsibility that weighed heavily on me as a landowner and farmer.

To encourage community wildlife on the farm, I used inputs (fertilizer, pest controls, seeds, water) that were not toxic. As I'll write about later, the soil life that had been damaged by anhydrous ammonia, a toxic fertilizer applied by the previous owner, returned when I used non-toxic inputs. Part of my master's research was useful here. During graduate school I had compared the effectiveness of several organic and conventional fertilizers. At the time, Iowa State University (ISU) horticulture professor Nick Christians made an interesting research observation quite by accident when he used corn meal to support a fungus he was studying in turf grass. The turf grass did not grow in the plot with the corn meal, and Christians discovered one component of it, corn gluten meal, inhibited root growth of sprouted seeds. The corn gluten meal became a useful natural weed control product that was patented by the university. Because it was also 10 percent nitrogen, it was a natural fertilizer as well. The discovery was of great interest to homeowners looking for natural inputs for their lawns, and was appealing to organic gardeners and farmers, also, because corn is a readily available raw material in the Upper Midwest. It seemed to be an ideal organic source of fertilizer and weed control for research I was conducting on strawberry production.

Like many organic farmers, I was concerned about the adverse effects of fertilizers on the soil community and my farm produce. I knew that a naturally derived, organic fertilizer was essential to the success of the CSA. But in the mid-1990s, synthetic fertilizers like urea were widely used in conventional agriculture. Urea is a white crystalline solid that contains 46 percent nitrogen. In 1995, with researchers from ISU, I conducted experiments in the farm fields and greenhouse that examined whether the nitrogen produced by corn gluten meal and composted turkey manure could replace urea in an organic system with strawberries—a crop that would be one of my customers' favorites. We found that depending on conditions, the organic sources of fertilizer could be as good as or better than urea and yielded quality strawberry crops during the month of June. In addition to using organic fertilizers, I supported the wildlife community on the farm in other ways by simply leaving them as they were—not unwittingly destroying bird nests, rodent tunnels, and insect habitat. Even though some of these community members could be a nuisance (ground squirrels eating our spinach, deer eating the lettuce), they were a part of the circle of life on the farm.

Engaging the wider human community in the farm was a bit more haphazard than my original simple triangle diagram. I used any opportunity to engage my customers, neighbors, and farming colleagues. The first annual event for customers was an orientation meeting before the season began, which gave me an opportunity to meet them, instruct them, answer questions on how the farm worked, and share a few prepared unusual foods like kohlrabi and edamame that they might see in their boxes in the future. Later in July we would have a garlic harvest and then an end-of-year potluck in September or October. Neighbors who lived close by had opportunities to visit the farm stand, harvest U-pick strawberries, and buy transplants. Field days at the farm were events that farming colleagues eagerly attended to learn about production practices or on-farm research.

Shortly after we purchased the farm, I got a grant from the Iowa nonprofit group Trees Forever for planting tree or bush crops in the farm's buffer zone—the thirty-foot space between the organic crop area and the adjacent nonorganic land of my neighbors as required by certification rules. I used this grant to purchase peach trees, hazelnut, elderberry, and red twig dogwood bushes. Crops from these plants in the buffer zone would not be considered organic, but the plants could still produce saleable crops and provide a barrier to potential chemical sprays. I invited my CSA customers as well as the new housing development neighbors next door to join together with the farm crew to plant these trees and bushes.

Dan Kopatich, one of my CSA customers, brought members of a local drumming group to the farm for the planting event. Each person's drum was a different size or shape. To me they seemed like large bongo drums. As the four men pounded the drums together, but not in unison, they gave a sense of formality to the planting process. It was a welcome call to Nature that only expected a living response in return, as if to say, "Join us in this growing adventure!" Some of the neighbors and their children came over to help. Theo, the son of one of my customers, had a broad smile on his face as he beat a large drum with his clenched fists, which made a deep vibration. His small legs could not begin to encircle the drum's radius. There was no worry about wrong notes, only pure joy and energy.

Engaging the wider community like this was easiest when I had U-pick strawberries available. Nothing is more popular than delicious, ripe berries. As a customer was paying for her harvest, she asked, "What else do you have for sale?"

"Well, all the rest of the produce is presold," I said, explaining the CSA concept. This single interaction gave me the impetus to pursue more community outreach. I began to sell excess produce at a stand on the farm twice a week. This did little more than pay for the helpers needed to run it, except during the popular berry season. Vegetables just don't have the same glamorous pull as fruit. I even gave five-dollar gift certificates to the neighbors in the development on our southern border as a way to meet them, to advertise the farm stand, to introduce them to organic farming, and to ask them to be careful with their lawn chemicals. No one ever cashed them in at the farm stand.

Outreach from the Granger community came one day when a woman involved in the local Catholic private school called me. "Would you consider having a children's garden for our preschool class?" she queried.

"I'll have to think about it," I said. I was excited at this chance to meet more of the local community and wanted to respond positively, but when we had previously attempted a garden for children of our CSA customers, it had had limited success. The biggest problem was the distance and time commitment for busy families. Hosting people who lived closer to the farm might be more successful, I reasoned. The farm crew and I gave it a try.

On planting day one dad asked, "What's a Brussels sprout?" He had never eaten one and did not know what it looked like. He looked bewildered as we started to plant them.

"Well, it's in the cabbage family. It's a tall stalk with baby cabbage-like balls on it," I tried to explain. The little transplants gave no clue to their final appearance.

"Here, these tomatoes need to be spaced several feet apart," I said to a young girl who was eager to plant as many as she could get in her plot. "When they grow up, they get big and needs lots of room." I guided her trowel to the proper spacing to dig a hole for her next tomato.

Next, I drew a furrow with my hoe in the plot to plant green beans. The children attacked the line with their trowels, digging further into the earth like they had done for the tomato transplants.

"Wait! These beans need to be planted closer to the surface so that they don't get lost, so that they can feel the warmth of the sun to help them push through the earth when they sprout," I instructed them. "Covering them with soil about the same depth as their width is a good rule of thumb for all seeds. And put the seeds this far apart." I showed them by holding my thumb and index finger two inches apart. The children backed off with their tools and dropped the seeds into the prepared furrow. We covered them gently but firmly with their hands and my hoe.

The second children's garden was more successful than the previous one had been. With the guidance of the preschool teacher and the closer proximity of the farm, the children along with helpers were able to visit the garden regularly to weed, water, and harvest the crops. The need for such an experience and education, for both the children and their parents, was obvious. Many of the things

I and other gardeners and farmers forget is how little the public might know about growing and eating the produce from a garden. Several of my customers had said they specifically signed up for the CSA so that their children could visit and see where their food came from. An entire generation or more has been divorced from the earth, giving up responsibility for their sustenance to others. If my triangular symbol of the CSA concept was any guide, these conversations with the children and parents were further proof that there was much work to be done, much support to be offered and given between farmers, consumers, and the places where we live.

Anything I could do to bring recognition to all the communities involved in this vital link to our soil, our food, and our ultimate survival became part of my goal. My mission was about more than growing healthy food. It was more holistic. It was about connecting all the interrelated forces bringing that food to the table so there was less separation between them. My focus became community wide.

6

THE "O" WORD

Organic farming appealed to me because it involved
searching for and discovering nature's pathways, as
opposed to the formulaic approach of chemical farming. The appeal of organic farming is boundless; this
mountain has no top, this river has no end.

ELIOT COLEMAN, *The New Organic Grower*

I HAD JUST FINISHED presenting my master's thesis seminar "Alternative Production Systems for Strawberries" at
Iowa State University before faculty and other students
in the Horticulture Department. It was shortly before my
graduation the summer of 1995. After presenting, my advisor asked me to take some paperwork to the administra-
tion building. It was a short walk on a pleasant summer
day, and I was relieved to have nothing stressful to do after
my presentation. On my way back, I encountered one of
the horticulture professors who had attended my seminar.
He slowed as we approached one another on the sidewalk,
looked up at me, and in a very matter-of-fact way said,
"Angela, I wouldn't pursue this organic thing if I were you."
I looked at him with surprise, having expected a compli-
ment or comment on my research. I waited a moment to
see if he would continue. He hadn't asked any questions or
made any comments during my seminar. He said nothing

more now. I didn't know how to respond, so I didn't. It wasn't the time or place for a discussion on the merits of organic versus conventional agriculture. He briskly turned aside and continued on his way.

I considered the professor's idea that I could drop "this organic thing." But by this point it was an integral part of me. It evolved through me as a value for life; it was what I and my family needed, and what the world and the environment needed. The foremost goal of any organic farm is a healthy environment rather than profit. Of course, organic farmers still need to make a profit to survive; that's part of being sustainable. I once had a person ask me if Turtle Farm was a nonprofit after learning about my organic farming venture. "Not intentionally," I replied. If one were to factor in the damage industrial agriculture does to the environment—pollution of waterways and oceans, degradation of soils, health risks associated with toxic chemicals for farmers and communities, and the production and use of fossil fuels for fertilizers that in turn affect ozone pollution and global warming—its profits wouldn't look as appealing. Instead, those costs are left to local communities to bear in the long term. We are all subsidizing that type of agriculture, twice if you add in government subsidies.

I first learned of organic agriculture from *Organic Gardening*, the garden-friendly magazine that greeted me at the grocery checkout lanes. Published by Rodale Press, its pages were full of practical information on alternative methods for growing food, as opposed to the prescribed fertilizer bags and bug sprays. Rodale also sponsored and reported on research that showed the benefits of organic gardening. For a backyard gardener like me in the 1970s and 1980s, some of the magazine's most useful features were submissions from readers of what was working in their home gardens.

In the 1980s the *Des Moines Register* printed a story that really caught my eye about an Iowa woman and her husband who were organic farmers. Denise O'Brian and Larry Harris began farming in 1976 on land his family owned for five generations. Denise also became a farm activist and later cofounded the Women, Food and Agriculture Network (of which I became a member) and ran for elective office. I watched her from afar with great interest and inspiration until I eventually met her, and we became friends.

Motherhood added to my interest in organic gardening. If I as a chemistry major could read the list of ingredients on a pesticide container and wonder about their effects on the life of an insect, how could I not wonder what effect they might have on a living human being? Why would I want to put this chemical on my food and feed it to my children? I wondered what chemicals and additives were being put in the food that I purchased from the grocery store (including the Apple Jacks my husband would surreptitiously buy and feed our children when I was out of town). Science was continually identifying problems with chemicals that had been previously approved and implemented for use in agriculture. But their synergistic effects—interactions with other chemicals that can make their effects more powerful—were only beginning to be assessed. There had to be a better and less risky way to grow food. This value drove my interest in organic farming, and it was and is driving the increase in demand for organic products everywhere.

Growing up on a farm, I certainly had seen my father use natural fertilizers with the manures that he collected from our animals. He would dig trenches to layer the aged manures below his tomato plants. And, yet, I had also seen him use insecticides on our summer squashes to repel bugs. I learned years later after I had left home, and my father had died from liver cancer, that my mother blamed some of the toxic chemicals he began to use on their farm for his illness.

Growing food organically with no synthetic fertilizers or pesticides was fairly easy to do in a manageable back-yard garden. Collecting yard clippings and food waste for a compost pile that could supply nutrients made a lot of sense. But doing it on a large scale was more complicated and assumed a holistic management of the full circle of nutrients that included animals, plants, and healthy soil. I had no animals, and I didn't live on the farm, which would have been necessary to manage them properly. Conditions at Turtle Farm were less than ideal in that regard. There were ways to procure compost, bring it to the farm, and use it that would meet the certified organic rules. But bringing in truckloads of compost wasn't always practical.

I attended a field day visit to Radiance Dairy Farm at Fairfield, Iowa, owned by Francis and Susan Thicke, organic farmers and Practical Farmers of Iowa members, where they expounded on the virtues of grass-fed cows. "Why expend all the human energy and fossil fuels to grow, cut, bale, and haul forages for the cows to the barn, when it is far easier and much more efficient to lead the cows to their food," Francis noted. To show us just what he meant, he headed down the dirt lane leading from the farm build-ings to a creek crossing and up the next hill. Without any encouragement, the Jersey cows, this smallest of dairy cattle breeds, fell in behind him and leisurely followed, tails swishing occasionally at flies. Their hooves clomping on the hard dirt surface was the only sound they made.

Francis came to a plot of knee-high, untouched mixed grasses and blooming clover enclosed in a single wire of electric fence. He stated that he changed the plot where the cows grazed each day, rotating through several different electric fence enclosures of about two acres each. He unclicked and pulled wide the wire gate and stood back, and the hungry cows, suddenly energized, rushed past him to get inside to begin feeding. It was easy to see how happy the cows were about this plan. They began devouring the fresh clovers and grasses with the help of their sandpaper-like black tongues and large white molars. They gazed back at us with "smiles" on their black and brown faces and contentment in their huge, dreamy brown eyes. Radiance, indeed! They left behind practical gifts of fertilizer just where it was needed.

I chose to follow the organic guidelines and become certified. Those who may follow organic guidelines but choose not to become certified cannot use the word "organic" to describe their product according to the National Organic Program (NOP). The certification is confirmed with an annual inspection, fees, and paperwork that details seed purchases, fertilizer and other inputs, water quality, methods of crop harvesting and storage, methods of land tillage, and rotations. Even though many consumers do not realize all the requirements of organic certification, which often took me a week in the winter to summarize on paper, I felt it would be a way to communicate my farming practices to those who were looking for healthy foods.

In June 2001, three years after the purchase of the farm, my phone rang. It was Maury Wills from the organic department of the Iowa Department of Agriculture and Land Stewardship (IDALS). Several weeks before, the organic certifier from IDALS had come to inspect the farm and greenhouse at my home. Maury was reporting the news, "Angela, you've passed the certification process, so you're good to go. We'll get the papers to you soon, but in the meantime, you can use the 'O' word freely." It was a big relief to pass our first certification. Since we bought the farm, it had had to wait three full years to become certified organic because it was previously farmed with pesticides and herbicides. During that time, I had used and documented organic practices per the requirements. We had started seeing results even in that short amount of time. There had been more and more earthworms as we worked in the soil, and more beneficial insects at work on some of the pests.

I educated my customers about organic practices through weekly newsletters and in person. Sometimes those of us doing the farming had a hard time keeping up with all the rules and changes, so one could not expect our consumers to always know the details. It may not have always made sense, but I explained as best I could. In 2006 I wrote:

> Some of the berries you may receive the rest of the summer will not be considered organic. "How can that be you ask—it's an organic farm?" Rules, rules, rules! When you purchase bare root perennial plants such as strawberries and raspberries that aren't organic (organic planting stock can be hard to find commercially), you have to wait one year of growth before they can be considered organic. There's no problem

with Junebearing strawberries as you plant them in the spring, they initiate flower buds in the short days of fall, and we harvest them in June of the next year, more than twelve months later. This year we hope to have some dayneutral strawberries produce in August and September, only six to seven months after planting because they can initiate their flowers buds in any day length. They were planted this year and will bear this year, so these dayneutral strawberries will not be considered organic.

If there were ever any questions about whether a farming practice—use of equipment, irrigation, crop rotation and storage, etc.—or inputs such as fertilizers or insect sprays on the farm qualified for being organic, farmers kept the phone lines buzzing with certifiers to get their opinion. Sometimes an input would get disallowed because of the way it was processed. This happened with the corn gluten meal that I had used in my master's research for a natural fertilizer because a solvent used to extract it was not approved. That was disappointing. When new products became available, we'd make a phone call to make sure that it was allowed within the certification before we used it. We didn't want to inadvertently make a mistake that would cost us three years for recertification.

An organic farm is subject to the surrounding farms that may be using sprays that are not allowed in organic farming. With possible drift of these chemicals in mind, one requirement for organic farms is to have a border between you and any nonorganic farm or property. This not only included the farm to the north of my property, but the housing development that eventually overtook the farm ground to the south. I could grow crops in this thirty-foot border, but they would not be considered organic.

I chose to grow cover crops of clovers and alfalfa and grasses that provided a great nursery for beneficial insects, bushes, and trees. It was alive with so many lady beetles, bumblebees, honeybees, and other insects that I hated to have to occasionally mow this great insectary. There were many kinds of lady beetles—dark red, dark orange, light orange, no spots, two spots, seven spots, some tiny, some robust. And yes, there were also cucumber and bean leaf beetles that one might consider pests. All were part of the balance that was our goal for the farm.

This border proved its value and protected us from sprays numerous times. We experienced more spray drift from lawn care companies to the south than from our conventional corn and soybean neighbor to the north. The companies were often unaware of wind speed or their customer's property lines in the housing development. As the number of organic farms has increased, there have been increasing numbers of these spray events. Some of my organic farmer colleagues lost the organic status of their crops because of these incidents and faced not only the reduced market price for their products in current and subsequent years, but the costs of litigation to try to recoup those losses as well.

The first year after we bought the farm, there was a warm April day, which allowed me to be at the property for some early season work. Since we had purchased twenty acres off of a ninety-nine-acre plot, the rest of the land that had not yet sold was still being farmed conventionally. A large tractor arrived with a sprayer attached, unfolded its "wings," and began to spray a preemergent herbicide on the bare ground. A preemergent is a spray that is put down before the crop that will be planted later and keeps weed seeds from sprouting and growing. As he worked his way across the adjoining land and came close to the boundary of our farm, I noticed there was enough wind that his spray was coming over onto my farm. The spray is not visible once it hits the ground, so at the ends of the "wings" of the sprayer, a white foam is emitted that helps the applicator see where he or she has sprayed. This foam was entering the border area of Turtle Farm. I immediately drove over to the adjoining land and caught the attention of the applicator. "Do you know what the wind speed is?" I yelled into the wind. "Your spray is coming onto my farm, and we're organic." Sprays are not to be applied if the wind speed is over ten miles per hour.

"I checked with the weather station before coming, and it's not over ten miles per hour," he replied. "Besides, it's just a preemergent." I wasn't so sure that the wind speed at that moment was only ten miles per hour, but I had no way to measure it and prove otherwise. I returned to the farm and kept a watchful eye on his spraying. His words "just a preemergent" displayed his lack of knowledge of what damage the spray could cause on my farm. I had broadcast clover seeds for a cover crop in March to frost seed it on part of the farm. This early spread of seed on top of the ground would eventually work its way into the soil in cracks that form from the freeze-thaw cycle when winter dissolves into spring, and then germinate and grow as spring progressed. By summer such a cover crop could be a foot high or more. It would produce nitrogen on its roots to fertilize the soil for the next season's crops and would further protect from erosion. A preemergent spray could prevent any seeds from sprouting, not just weeds. I held my breath until the cover crop came up that spring. Luckily his spray had not reached beyond the border.

A more welcome encounter with a neighbor came later.

As an organic farmer, I needed to inform my neighbors to be careful of sprays around my property. Bob Sturgeon, owner of Barr-Nunn Trucking, whose headquarters lay across the highway, had recently purchased the rest of the land south of the farm. I visited him at his office in Granger to ask that his farmers be careful with sprays. He was cordial, and I left feeling he had at least heard my concerns. Two days later he drove up to the barn as we were having lunch. I stepped outside to speak with him. "Angela, I spoke with the farmer that I've hired who is going to be working the ground next to you. We've decided to put in twenty-seven acres of alfalfa. Would that be all right?" he asked. "That sounds great," I replied. After a few more pleasantries regarding the vegetables we were growing, he left. Inwardly I was rejoicing! No corn and soybeans to be planted and sprayed or heavily fertilized next to the farm was a gift. At that time, alfalfa was rarely sprayed. I was very grateful to Bob Sturgeon for those few years that alfalfa grew next to the farm.

All the rules in the NOP are concerned with safety. In 2006 there was a spinach contamination outbreak from E. coli on an organic farm in California. How could this happen? In this case it was eventually learned that the E. coli was found in nearby cattle fields and in a wild boar that was killed in one of the spinach fields. This incident resulted in better practices for growing and harvesting of leafy greens in California. Such events help us all to learn and fine-tune our production methods. That was certainly a concern for me and my customers.

With the concern over the contaminated spinach, one of my customers emailed a question. "I had a friend ask me what organic crops were fertilized with. She asked if you use manure, and I said I didn't know. Then she asked, if manure was used, was there a greater threat of getting sick from E. coli and other bacteria?"

I responded to her, "Health crises like the spinach recall make us all think more about how our food is grown, so I am happy to answer you and your friend's questions as best I can." I explained that E. coli and other bacteria are naturally occurring in the soil. Probably the biggest problem is that with the overuse of antibiotics in animals, a resistant superstrain of E. coli has emerged. And since manures are a primary source of E. coli, their management is very important.

I added that organic farmers cannot use synthetic fertilizers. There are a variety of things we do use. These might include compost, legumes (sometimes called a green manure), cover crops, fish emulsion, worm castings, and minerals as needed. Organic and conventional farmers can both use manures, but organic farmers are restricted in how they use them—they cannot be used within four months of harvest so that they have a chance to break down, which means they are generally put down in the fall and incorporated at the same time for vegetable farmers. In addition, we are required to have our water sources tested annually for E. coli and nitrates.

I went on to inform her about what I used at Turtle Farm. I spoke of the uncontrolled "applications" that we all have to watch out for. The wildlife—wandering deer, raccoons, birds, coyotes—can cross any farm at any time. We were always on the watch for droppings and avoided harvesting produce in those areas. Runoff from animal farms was also a concern, so organic farmers must be aware of those possible contamination spots as well. My farm was well situated so that was not a problem.

Another time I had a contamination concern that scared

me come up in a conversation with a customer at a pickup site. She said her son had been sick and that the doctors thought it might be food poisoning. With my heart in my throat, I summoned the courage to ask if it might have been from my produce. She looked at me a bit surprised, broke into a smile and laughed, and said, "No, I can't get him to eat your vegetables, Angela." Never had I thought that those words could be so comforting.

7

WAITING OUT THE STORM

On cable TV they have a weather channel—twenty-four
hours of weather. We had something like that where I
grew up. We called it a window.
—DAN SPENCER

I GREW UP IN THAT REGION of the Midwest known as tornado alley, but I've never seen or experienced a tornado.
For the rest of my life, regardless of where I lived, tornado
warnings would remind me of my early years in Oklahoma. I vividly remember being awakened as a six-year-
old during a stormy summer night, but not by the storm.

"Get up, Angela! Hurry up! We've got to get downstairs,"
my older sister Rosa Lee said, shaking my shoulder. My
sister Charlotte pulled off the sheet in the sticky air.

"David, Danny, get up!" my mother called in the next
bedroom.

It was dark, I wasn't fully awake, and I was confused. We
felt our way down the dark stairway as quickly as we could
be herded. My brothers and sisters and I hurried past the
front door.

"CRACKLE—CRASH—BOOM!" A bolt of lightning jarred
us to a standstill and illuminated the dark house. I could
see the silhouette of my father dressed only in his boxer

shorts and T-shirt standing in the doorway. He was intently watching the storm. It was the early 1950s, and we had no TV or radar to consult.

"Let's go!" he said suddenly. The cellar was only fifty feet from the kitchen door. My father led the way through the house and out the back door, dashing barefoot off the porch into the muddy yard and rain. He stopped and pulled open the creaky, wooden doors of the cellar against the force of the strong wind. "Come on!" he yelled at us.

Mother brought up the rear with my youngest brother, Dan, while shooing us forward. We dashed barefoot through the sloshy mud and horizontal sheets of pelting rain, finding our way in flashes of lightning. I'm sure my sisters were pushing me forward ahead of them because I arrived at the cellar first.

I set my first foot into the dark, dank opening. "There's water on the floor," I whined. "Aaack! Spider webs!" I screamed as they snagged body parts. I imagined the actual spiders crawling on me, but I couldn't dwell on it. My family pushed and shoved me further into the darkness. The minute we were inside, my father jumped into the cellar behind us and pulled the doors closed behind him. We huddled there in the cool darkness, relieved to be safe until the storm passed, relieved that it hadn't been a tornado.

Living in tornado alley made me appreciate and respect the weather. One could easily see the weather approach on the flat plains of Grady County, Oklahoma. In the Upper Midwest, the weather generally approaches from the west. I feel deprived—almost claustrophobic—if I can't see to the west from my home. When my husband John and I lived in Virginia, the numerous hardwood trees were too tall for a view of the horizon, and in our current house, we only have an easterly view. But Turtle Farm had a great western view, and somehow it was a comfort, informative, and at times exciting.

Wind, hail, late spring frost, and floods can be devastating weather events for a farm. The diversity of crops on a CSA farm is one form of insurance for keeping a good supply of produce in the box each week. Growing more than thirty fruit and vegetable crops in hundreds of varieties is part of that insurance plan. If one or two or even three crops fail, my customers might not even notice. But customers definitely noticed when favorites like the strawberry crop were touched by frost. Some crops such as green beans, summer squash, and cucumbers ripened quickly enough that a second or third succession could be planted if the first failed. Low and high tunnels were being used more and more by farmers in an attempt to buffer the weather's unpredictable nature. These tunnels were temporary structures of long, clear plastic sheets pulled over wire hoops and a bed of crops that were three to five feet high. But a hailstorm or tornado could be a devastating blow that a farm might not recover from even with the insurance of diverse crops.

Communication with my customers about the weather was an important part of educating them about the consequences of what was happening at the farm. After all, the weather was impacting their investment in their farm and food. It also impacted working outdoors for the farm crew. The workday might be delayed because of rain or started and ended earlier by high heat. We kept a weather radio at the farm just for those occasions when we needed up-to-date information on what was happening or about to happen. During one spring storm in 2010, we turned it on as we saw storm clouds gathering.

"NNGGG! NNGGG! NNGGG!" The obnoxious, computer-generated buzzer on the weather radio preceded its weather warnings. A storm was approaching and all seven of us, the farm crew and me, were inside the barn. We had been able to harvest the crops for the day's deliveries before the threatening weather approached. We huddled in the small space of the farm stand, a twelve-by-eight-foot room with large, wooden shutters, and calmly bagged peas and lettuce. Occasionally we would cast our eyes to the window where we could see the dark clouds approaching from the west. Doug Nichols had coincidentally stopped by for a visit. Doug had single-handedly built my barn one summer a few years earlier. Its solid structure gave me comfort as a safe place to be. Before that I only had a canvas canopy, the hoop house, and the cooler for shelter—all with metal frames that were not safe for an Iowa lightning storm. We would use our vehicles for safe shelter in those days if lightning threatened. The sturdy countertops that Doug had constructed in the farm stand were so strong, I would have ducked under them in an emergency. Six employees were another matter.

"A line of storms is moving eastward in a line stretching from O-MA-ha to Fort Dodge," the weather radio continued with its warnings. "O-MA-ha" we echoed back at the radio. We always laughed at the computer-generated pronunciation of Omaha. We continued with our small talk as we worked. The farm crew quizzed Doug on the location of the nickel he put in every structure as his signature tradition. They guessed that it was embedded in the concrete under the wooden shelving.

The next weather warning said the storm was getting much closer. We could see the sky darken even more into a wall cloud in the distance and, beyond that, rain on the horizon several miles away with thunder growing closer and closer. Sue spoke up. "What will we do if there's a tornado?"

I laid out two options. "Bob and Michelle Fitch in the housing development next to the farm and Marcia and Merle Hall in town have basements."

Just as I was about to make a phone call to arrange shelter, lightning crackled and the accompanying jolt and loud thunder let us know the storm was overhead. Rain began in torrents, and the sky turned from black to gray. The rain unleashed intense energy in the air. It wasn't too long before the sky brightened, and the sun peeked through thinning clouds. The weather radio announced new coordinates of the severe storm that had gone north of our area. Meanwhile, our packing work had ended. The general rule is to stay indoors thirty minutes past a lightning strike, so we sat in the farm stand and made a list of everything we needed to do when the time was up.

When people ask me what my biggest challenge is in organic farming, I assume they expect it to be things like weeds and insects since I don't use pesticides. I always answer "The weather." Weather can impact just about everything on a farm, even the weeds and insects. When there is wet ground, farmers can't get in to weed the crops, and those weeds can quickly steal nutrients and moisture, overtaking the crops if the ground doesn't dry out quickly enough.

Insect populations are sometimes high because of winter snow cover, which can protect them. In 2012 there was a huge explosion of leaf hopper insects after unusual spring southern winds blew them in from the South. Their normal food wasn't available, so they latched onto the few things they could find that were green that early in the season, which turned out to be garlic at Turtle Farm and many other vegetable farms in the region. This led to aster yellows (a disease caused by a phytoplasma bacteria spread by the leaf hoppers when they chew on the plants) developing in our garlic. We'd never seen this in garlic before. In the past, garlic had always been an easy, pest-free crop to grow. Later we noticed spots on the leaves, sometimes browning tips, sometimes stunted growth. One particular characteristic was a slight smoky smell to the garlic that might otherwise look normal. We spent a lot of time sniffing garlic before we placed the bulbs in our CSA boxes that season. Aster yellows made a lot of the garlic unmarketable and a poor choice to use for our own planting stock for the next season. Both of those losses were financially painful.

My farming challenges have been split between those I could control and those I could not. Weather that can bring drought or floods, windstorms or hail, has always been outside a farmer's control. I tried to make some mitigating choices, such as irrigation, to lessen those effects and to improve the odds of survival.

Irrigation for vegetable farmers is essential. Vegetables are 90 percent water, whereas the moisture content of Upper Midwest grain crops such as corn and soybeans are closer to 30 and 15 percent respectively at harvest. Average rainfall in the region is usually sufficient for these row crops to be grown without the need for irrigation. The first improvement at our newly purchased farm was a deep well—a very expensive investment. Irrigation was an important consideration in deciding which crops, how much to grow, and where to grow them. So, when the well driller gave me a choice, I knew the answer.

"I've found water at fifty feet," he said. "Do you want me to keep drilling?"

I asked whether that was going to be enough to water an acre of ground at a time.

"Probably not in a drought year," he replied.

I also knew that a fifty-foot well would not keep out surface contaminants that could seep through that much soil. "Keep drilling," I said. We eventually found good pressure and water at six hundred feet. I never experienced a shortage of water from that well.

In a drought, I looked to the weather forecasts every day for signs of rain. It was frustrating to hear the cheery local weather forecasters praise the beautiful weather we were having when every day without rain was an ugly day at the farm. These people were definitely not connected to their local food sources. After all, grocery stores were packed with a bounty that seemed to just magically appear. It made me marvel once again at our ancestors who had to grow their own food or do without. How well would we do in that setting now?

When I hoped for rain every day, any signs of it arriving drew my attention. But, especially in drought years, the fickle nature of Iowa weather could be disappointing. One harvest day in June 2006, before we could begin gathering crops, it began to lightning at the farm. We sat in the barn for an hour and a half waiting for the flashes to end. We only got sprinkles. Customers called to see if we had received rain, but what little there was had gone south that day. That dry spring many of the crops that I grew had gotten all their significant moisture from irrigation that was running almost constantly.

The total rainfall for May that year had been 1.2 inches, and for June 0.15 inches. Average rainfall for Iowa in May and June would have been 4.7 and 4.9 inches respectively. When relief came in July, the reduction of stress on both the farm workers and produce was palpable. You could almost hear the plants and animals sighing with relief and soaking it all in. I sat with John in our sunroom as we ate our dinner that evening after the wonderful rain.

"Look," I said. "Do you see the twin fawns up the driveway there?" We often saw deer at our home, which was surrounded by woods. "They're splashing and playing in those water puddles like little kids. It's like they've never seen one before." They were almost dancing in the puddles, raising their legs and stomping their hooves in the water, their heads lowered to watch the effect of it all. There had not been enough rain in the fawns' short lifetimes the past two months to even generate puddles.

Drought years are often accompanied with high heat, creating a double whammy for farmers. Helping the farm crew mitigate the heat meant early morning start times and often ending the workdays earlier than usual. We might spend days hauling out the trickle irrigation lines— thin, black tubes of plastic with tiny holes at intervals to allow water to seep out—and hours moving them around the farm to different locations.

There are challenges to dealing with cold weather as well. One October as our season was nearing its end, it was so cold and windy even the critters were bewildered. A sparrow exhausted from fighting the wind flew into the farm stand as we were packing boxes on a delivery day to just sit and rest for a bit. It was too tired to be afraid of us. Normally we would have chased any bird out of the packing area, but this day we empathized and let it be. Two salamanders strolled into the farm stand at different times the same day. We rarely saw the reclusive Eastern tiger salamanders at the farm, but when we did, it was usually because we had accidentally uncovered their shady, cool hiding places. Salamanders don't move very fast on a warm day. On this cold day they crept along like molasses, and it was only sheer luck and their yellow spots that allowed us to see them.

Wind and frost and flooding are also hard to deal with, but there are still factors farmers can implement for some protection. Some of the mitigation efforts that I relied on were as simple as deciding which land to purchase (not in total lowlands) or where on that land to plant a certain crop. A gentle slope allows cold, frosty air to flow downward, so crops that were most subject to spring frost, such as strawberries or fruit trees, I planted on a slope or just above it.

Frost protection in addition to planting on or above slopes included covering our strawberries with Reemay (a synthetic ground cloth), which didn't work very well for an acre of ground. We would spread out the cloths and staple them down, but the wind would often catch them like a sail and send them flying. We found ourselves repeating the process many times in the dark by the light of my truck headlights once the wind had settled down.

Overhead irrigation is a better option for saving berries from frost. The transition of water turning to ice—called latent heat of fusion—gives off some warmth that can prevent the blossoms from freezing. If the frost duration time is long, however, the fields can get flooded from the constant irrigation, and wet soil can cause other problems. Turtle Farm didn't use this method because it required a large investment in infrastructure.

Some of the best protection from wind comes from strategically placed trees or bushes. A tree or bush or even a building can buffer wind for a distance of two and a half times its height. Of course, these are long-term solutions, but they are a consideration when purchasing land. Temporary buffers such as stacks of hay bales or even a fence can have a wind buffering effect on smaller areas. But it's hard to have buffers in the middle of large fields. The leaves of our summer and winter squashes can and did act like sails in stiff winds and broke off when being whipped about in sixty-mile-per-hour gales.

As for flooding, low-lying sites along creeks or natural drainage areas can have good, light, loamy soils comprised of equal parts sand, silt, and clay for vegetables, but any farmer must offset that choice of planting site with what could happen if a torrential rain drops inches of water in a short amount of time. It's a gamble without a crystal ball, and one day in August 2010, a year that had more than its share of moisture problems, that gamble did not go our way. The sky had dumped several inches of rain in a short amount of time late that afternoon. I had gone home and checked the radar often to see what it was doing at the farm ten miles away. Then a phone call came from Ben.

"We got four inches here at the farm," he said.

"How bad is it?" I asked tentatively. I knew he wouldn't have called unless there was a problem.

"I think you better come see for yourself," he replied.

The fifteen-minute drive to Granger couldn't go fast enough. When I arrived at the entrance to the farm, Ben was there in his vehicle. The worst of the flooding was right in front of us where the lower ground was ten to fifteen feet below. The drainage ditches at the road were unable to handle the amount of water that flowed down the gentle slopes of our farm and the other nearby areas. The power of the moving water was staggering as it rushed over part of our lower crop area and washed out sixty feet of gravel as it flowed over the driveway. We saw a rabbit and frogs swimming with all their strength amid the submerged crops. The sight was sickening, but there was nothing we could do. We just sat in painful silence calculating the damage in our minds.

The next day as we surveyed the fields, we found three beds of newly planted crops that were washed out. There would not be time to replant the fall carrots, beets, and spinach for the CSA—they were a total loss. It was painful to see how much topsoil had been lost in areas that only had subsoil showing now. I had planted perennial grass, strawberries, and raspberries horizontally across the gentle slopes on the farm to hold the soils back in heavy rainfall. I knew of no way to stop this river running horizontally across the lowest part of the farm.

The next day we also discovered a log in our onion patch, which was not even at the lowest area of the farm. Apparently, it had come from the tiny creek along the north side of the property that had overflowed from a log jam of debris at a bend in the creek. The next week brought us an additional 8.5 inches of rain spread out over days. The farm was like a swamp. We harvested that onion patch where we found the log. It was one of the few things we could do in the mud. As we pulled each one out, the saturated ground formed a vacuum, made a suction noise, and the holes filled with water in the round, vacated space. Drying out those onions in the sun was not enough to prevent mold growing under their skins later. They were usable, but they were not considered good keepers. The tomatoes split and molded easily, almost before we could send them out in the customer boxes. We communicated these and other issues to the CSA members so that our customers would understand potential quality and quantity issues with their vegetables. Most of my customers understood how the weather affected their food, but it was still a moment I had hoped not to experience. Not being able to fulfill a promised harvest on this scale felt like a gut-wrenching failure.

Disappointment went hand in hand with catastrophic weather events. Sometimes farms are not able to financially brave severe devastations. But in these rough times, the support of the CSA customers was a needed buffer for me. Each had signed up to support Turtle Farm through bounty and bust. The good times kept us going—highlights that I made sure to point out each week, even despite the problems. Got floods? Look at all the abundant tree frogs who will eat insects. There would be more vegetables and better weather in our future. Our farm would recover. Just as my family had sat in that damp cellar many years before waiting out the storm, we endured, but we didn't surrender.

8

THE WISDOM
OF BIODIVERSITY

The snake stitches together the ecosystem like a thread
through cloth: unobtrusive, beautiful, and effective: a
symbol of the wisdom of nature indeed.
—JEREMY HOLDEN, "Standing Up for Snakes" (Fauna &
Flora International, fauna-flora.org)

THE INFLUENTIAL BIOLOGIST E. O. WILSON calls biodiversity "our most valuable but least appreciated resource."
Biodiversity is an important consideration for any farm,
but especially farms that operate under the model of
community-supported agriculture (CSA). A biodiverse environment can save soils from erosion with cover crops, allow
biological control to balance pest populations, and help
whole ecosystems to function and thrive in an intercon-
nected web. It is a model that fits nicely with the cooperative
CSA philosophy. CSA farms typically grow a wide variety of
crops so that most will survive even if there are pest inva-
sions or extreme weather. Monocrop farms are more vulnerable to drastic losses if they encounter the wrong pest,
adverse weather, or economic supply-and-demand issues.
Biodiverse farms thrive by living in harmony with wildlife
and interweaving their production in ways that make use

of many resources, such as raising animals on pasture eating a natural diet of different grasses rather than confining them to a grain-based diet in a feedlot. Those grasses foster biodiversity with microbe, insect, bird, and mammal populations, especially if they are native or prairie grasses; barren dirt feedlots aren't nearly as effective.

Everywhere I look there are signs that humans try to push Nature to the edge. We can see it in expansive industrial farms, in housing developments that scrape up everything in their path and then lay a little soil back down to grow turf grass, and in urban high-rises that leave little around them but concrete. Parks are helpful in many ways but may not be large enough to support true biodiversity. Adding native plants that support biodiverse life to parks, lawns, and farms could make an impactful difference in sustaining these environments.

Large conservation areas are unquestionably necessary for bigger species—bison, elk, and caribou. But Douglas Tallamy, a professor of entomology and wildlife ecology, in his book *Nature's Best Hope* (2019), explains discovering that certain insects need a surprising amount of space to flourish. A carabid beetle, for example, needs twenty acres to flourish and successfully reproduce. The same is true for some bird species. What role can a farm play in fostering biodiversity?

Research by the Iowa State University Science-based Trials of Row-crops Integrated with Prairie Strips (STRIPS) program shows just how much effect even small conservation practices can have on working row-crop farms where there is little biodiversity. STRIPS are 10 percent of a farm area and consist of perennial plantings of prairie grasses and forbs that reduce water runoff, sediment, and nutrient losses by significant amounts. CSA farming colleague Gary Guthrie who participated in the study with his farm in Story County reported ninety-two native bee species and a large variety and quantity of birds, some of which had not been seen on the property before. The program has been so successful that it has extended into thirteen states beyond Iowa. For farmers, STRIPS is a good step forward for biodiversity.

When we purchased our twenty-acre property, it had previously been farmed conventionally using anhydrous ammonia. It's incredibly common as a fertilizer on Upper Midwestern cropland because it's relatively inexpensive, and farmers can inject it into the soil in the fall to reduce their spring workload. Anhydrous ammonia is highly caustic because of its great affinity for water. It will burn human skin (or lungs if inhaled) and can severely damage soil life (bacteria, fungi, and earthworms) in the vicinity of the application. But here, too, a symphony of new life can begin with the rehabilitation of land when one stops using chemical fertilizers and pesticides. You can imagine my excitement when we began to see new life in the soil. It was August of the first year on the farm. Kristen Vetterlein, my only employee that year, and I were digging potatoes. She was using a spading fork, unearthing one hill of potatoes at a time. I was kneeling on the ground to collect the spuds and place them all in a crate as we worked.

"Look!" I exclaimed peering down at the black soil. "An earthworm!" A good sign.

"The first one we've seen all season!" Kristen gushed. I handed it up to her. We admired it like a rare zoo animal.

We would eventually find four more earthworms that season. In following seasons we found them in every hole we dug as the soil life recovered.

Earthworms are an important part of the soil ecosystem. Their tunnels provide pores that allow water and oxygen to infiltrate the soil and carbon dioxide to escape. They eat their weight in organic matter every day, providing nutrients to plant roots while at the same time improving soil structure through their droppings, known as castings. Ground-dwelling insects, bacteria, protozoa, amoebas, and even small mammals contribute similar benefits.

Turtle Farm hosted a wide variety of wildlife that increased in numbers as the years went by. The flora and fauna of any farm can differ greatly from another farm or it can be different in different years on the same farm depending on the weather. For instance, in wetter years, our farm had lots of leopard frogs—also known as meadow frogs. This was probably because of the proximity of a swampy pond at the top of a nearby hill, the stream down the north side of the property, and the inclination of water to linger in the ditch at the highway. Leopard frogs need a water environment to hatch their eggs. Adults are often found on dry ground and help keep insect populations at bay.

Tree frogs, on the other hand, were everywhere but the ground. They would try to blend in with their camouflage colors on our red farm equipment or the shady white sides of the barn. More often we would discover them among the plants where they would feast on insects. It's a real treat to pull aside a raspberry branch and discover a tiny tree frog quietly blending into the flora. They ranged from thumbnail size to as big as a silver dollar. We also had our toads, our large bull snakes, many, many mice, and a wonderful bird population. Footprints in the mud told of evening visitors—coyote, deer, skunks, and especially raccoons in the corn.

Birds were the most common wildlife that we encountered at the farm. Each spring, bluebirds and meadowlarks were the first to entertain us with their songs, and we welcomed their worm- and bug-eating habits. During spring planting, the birds were also busy tending their "crops," consuming vast numbers of insects and worms for their offspring. We found nests in a row of trellised peas, in among the raspberry bushes, and woven around the garlic scapes. As we picked our way through their nurseries, we were cautious not to disturb them. Because nests could be on the ground hidden in the grass or even in the wide-open spaces, we took care to not mow the meadow until the end of June when nesting season was over.

Birds can be very persistent in their choice of housing, and we would sometimes repeatedly remove the beginnings of nests that were started in inappropriate places. Swallows often wanted to build their muddy nests above the barn's bathroom door. Every year a robin built a nest in the open motor housing of our cooler. We would remove nests like these unless they already had eggs in them. Once the eggs were laid, we tried to cooperate with the birds by leaving the nests alone. But when the barn was being built, we had to take extraordinary measures.

"Angela, we have a problem," Doug Nichols said to me one morning. Doug had almost finished the barn. "See that robin's nest up on that rafter?" He pointed to the middle of the high rafter running under the roof. You could just barely see the nest. "She thinks she's found a great protected spot there, but it's not going to work out once we put the window in. Those babies are going to be stuck in here."

The farm crew and I considered the options we had for preserving this robin family. And luckily, Doug was a kindhearted guy who was game for our solution. We proposed moving the nest over toward the window ten feet at a time across the rafter so that she could still find it when she flew in to feed the babies. Doug gladly got a ladder and proceeded to move the nest every hour or so closer to the window where the mother robin found the nest successfully each time. For the final step, Doug inserted the window in the mother's absence and put the nest up on a special window ledge he constructed on the outside of the window, placing a piece of cardboard behind the nest so that the mother bird's reflection in the glass would not startle her. It worked! That robin family carried on as if nothing had ever threatened their existence that day.

Humans can certainly be a dangerous hazard for new bird life. One spring afternoon, the farm crew was out in the field weeding tomatoes. A killdeer or sandpiper was shrieking at us to express its discontent with our presence. Usually these birds feign injury, drag a wing, and try to lure you away from the nest. But this no-nonsense bird was adamantly guarding its territory. Their nests are so barren and camouflaged that I have been known to step in one in the past. This time we spotted the simple stick nest with four brown-splotched tan eggs under a young tomato plant right beside the protective, noisy bird. We obeyed the frantic parent and moved away, placing a red flag stake by the tomato later so that we would remember not to weed it—there were plenty of other weeds to tend to. One month later we saw cute little puffballs on long, stick legs running after their parents.

Birds were highly visible at the farm, but other animals were not so obvious. When the ground on the south side of our land was being developed, some of my visiting customers commented on the changes that might bring to our farm. This was generally talked about in the context of new customers, more litter and noise, and the increasing value of the farmland. But as the housing development took shape, I noticed more subtle changes in the wildlife. The deer visited less frequently. Pheasants that we often heard and sometimes met in the raspberries taking dust baths seemed to disappear. I saw more rabbits, which I attributed to a reduced presence of the coyotes.

Soon after we purchased the farm, I stayed late one evening to meet a beekeeper who wanted to put a hive on the grounds. It was then that I first heard our coyote neighbors howling at dusk. I never saw a coyote on the farm, but they made their presence known in other ways. One year I noticed wooden garden stakes pulled out of the ground and displaced in the paths. Plastic trickle irrigation lines showed signs of being chewed on by an animal with sharp teeth. I began to suspect a coyote. That fall I was planting the garlic bed and came to the end of the day. I had not yet finished with the chore, so it seemed efficient to leave the measuring tape and trowel in the bed to mark my place. The next morning the one-hundred-foot measuring tape was strung halfway up the hill, and my favorite trowel was gone. My first thought was a two-footed thief, but I found only dog tracks in the surrounding dirt. I'm still waiting for the return of the borrowed tool.

Encounters with our wildlife friends were almost always enjoyed by the farm crew, but there were some repeat offenders. Deer, squinnies (thirteen-lined ground squirrels), rabbits, and a few insects were the most obvious herbivores that might frustrate us. It was rare that anyone on the farm crew actually liked the snakes, which irrationally scare some people just by their presence. In the case of one employee, Angelique Hakuzimana from Rwanda, Africa, where there are only poisonous snakes, perhaps it was a rational fear. I did have an employee one year who was an amateur herpetologist. Imagine my surprise when he went to his car and retrieved a snake hook to catch and relocate a snake we found in our raspberry patch.

I might be startled by snakes, but I appreciate their worth to the biodiversity on a farm. Snakes eat mice. Mice eat weed seeds, which is a benefit, but they also eat our potatoes, sweet potatoes, and tomatoes. The snakes help keep rodent populations in check. We had had at least four species on the farm. One day I heard excited screaming up the hill where the crew was digging sweet potatoes. I thought they were elated about the size of the produce, but it turns out they had dug up a nest of ring-necked snakes. Adults only grow to ten to fourteen inches long; they looked like a mass of baby snakes swarming about the ground.

Bull snakes were the predominant species at the farm. We would often see them in the early spring in the asparagus patch basking in the warm sun on the straw mulch. Though they might be six to eight feet long, they seemed to have no awareness of their own bodies. We would use bird netting to cover the crops that were favored by deer— lettuce, beets, Swiss chard. The bull snakes could get their heads through the three-quarter-inch mesh, but the rest of their bodies were too large, and they would become stuck. They couldn't move forward or back out because their scales would catch in the plastic mesh. One harvest morning Sue, Ben, and I had gone out to pull beets. Ben noticed it first.

"There's a snake skeleton down here," he said as he removed one side of the mesh that covered the beets.

"Oh, I can smell it!" Sue said as she made a face.

"That's been here a while," I commented. "I hate it when our good intentions kill critters." These reptiles were an important part of the farm ecosystem, and we didn't want to be the cause of their demise. "We need to start scouting the covered crops daily, so we can free them before they die." Everything has consequences. In our human-made gardens, sometimes our manipulations don't always turn out the way we intended for the benefit of crops and wildlife.

The most memorable time we rescued a snake was one harvest day morning. I was picking the Swiss chard. We had covered it with bird netting to ward off the deer. As I pulled out the staples to open one side of the netting, I saw a four-foot-long bull snake caught in it. It was still alive. I went to get Ben for another pair of hands to help. "Ben, we've got another snake in the netting. Can you help me remove it?" I asked.

"Sure, let me get my clippers," he said, and he ran to the farm stand. I met him in the chard patch. Ben bravely held the snake's writhing body as he cut away the netting caught around its head. I made myself useful by holding the netting to provide tension for Ben to cut more easily. "Just one more string of the plastic to cut now," he said.

Just at that moment, the snake began to convulse. Its jaws opened wide and almost appeared to unhinge exposing its pink mouth and fangs. We jerked to attention wondering if it was going to attempt to bite us. No! Rather it immediately regurgitated a dark object about three inches long. Ben and I looked at each other in wide-eyed amazement.

"Oh, my gosh!" I said. "Do you see that? It's a mouse! You can still see its dark fur and tail!"

"I've never seen anything like that before," Ben said shaking his head, but before he could respond further, the snake opened its jaws wide again and regurgitated another object like the first, slightly more digested, but still recognizable as a mouse. "I don't believe this!" he said. "That blows my mind." He spoke for both of us.

We released the snake, happy that it was alive, sad that it had lost its breakfast, and impressed with the very visible, tangible, and rewarding effects of our farm ecosystem at work. We knew the population-balancing results of diversity happened in theory, quietly, and out of sight, but it was a once in a lifetime event to see actual evidence of them like this.

9

THAT BUG ON YOUR PLATE

If all mankind were to disappear, the world would regenerate back to the rich state of equilibrium that existed ten thousand years ago. If insects were to vanish, the environment would collapse into chaos.

—E. O. WILSON

IN LATE JUNE 2007 I got a call at the farm from research entomologist James Cane in Utah. "Hi, Angela, I got your name from the Iowa State University (ISU) entomology department. I'm going to be in Ames next week for an international conference on Colony Collapse Disorder. I was wondering if you have summer squash in bloom?"

I was deep in "hoeing meditation," but I directed my thoughts to my squash, which we had just started picking the previous week. "Yes," I replied, "I have blooms, but I don't sell them if that is what you are interested in." I didn't want to decrease yields in my crop by removing the blossoms. Male squash blossoms that do not become fruit are often picked and sold to restaurants for stuffing. They're important for pollination of the female blossoms, which do become the fruit. He continued, "No, I wouldn't buy them. I was wondering if I could visit your farm since it's not too far from Ames and look for squash bees. They're a native, ground-dwelling bee, most likely here pollinating the squashes of Native Americans way before the Europeans brought over the honeybee. We wouldn't disturb your plants, just look for the bees."

It sounded like an interesting and educational proposal, so I agreed. When James and another researcher from England came the next week, they did indeed find *Peponapis pruinosa* buzzing about. This was the first I had heard of such a native bee. When they pointed it out to me, it was flying so fast that it looked like any other small bee. I had to Google it later to get a better look. These little honeybee-sized insects pollinate the squash family exclusively. They are probably part of the reason that I hadn't noticed a difference in squash production between times when there was or wasn't a European honeybee hive at the farm. Because *Peponapis pruinosa* builds its nests in the ground and eats nectar and pollen, it is especially vulnerable to pesticides used in squash crops. For me insects and other forms of wildlife were a part of the "community" of our community-supported agriculture venture. Using organic practices would ensure that they would continue to be an essential part of the farm.

Part of my preparation for farming at ISU was a class in entomology. John Obrycki, a professor and a member of my graduate research team, guided me through one of the hardest classes I had ever taken—Biological Control, a graduate-level course on beneficial insects. I had no background in entomology, even as an undergraduate, so I was starting out at a disadvantage. During our first test on tiny, beneficial insect identification, I was in a bit of a panic as they all looked alike, even under the microscope! I was still learning the basic body parts but was much relieved when it was announced that it would be an open-book test. My relief turned back to panic when I learned there were special, two-week courses at another university that graduate students could attend to learn to identify these insects. Somehow, I survived that class and came to appreciate the wide variety of beneficial insects working in our world, many of which we can barely see.

In Biological Control, I learned that a problem with a pest can often be the result of an insect that has been transported to a new area where its natural predator is not located. To solve these pest problems, the missing beneficial insect is sometimes brought to the location of the pest, and a new balance might be restored. Historically, this often happened when pests arrived from other countries by accident. I would often use the method of biological control to determine which natural predators were missing when pests began to show up at the farm. Got rabbits? Most likely their natural predator coyotes have been displaced from the area by human invasion. Some cats and dogs could partially fill this void, but in an urban area with fenced yards, it can be difficult to resolve. Part of the solution at the farm was to keep weeds and tall grasses mowed so that the rabbits had fewer places to hide, and the coyotes could be more successful in finding their prey. Mice galore? Coddle the snakes if possible. The people whose first instinct is to kill a snake they find in their yard may not relate the occurrence to the invasion of mice in their homes later in the season. Caterpillars a problem? The naturally occurring bacterium *Bacillus thuringiensis (Bt)* is an approved organic biological control for caterpillars that is frequently used by vegetable growers. These bacteria contain a toxic protein that destroys a caterpillar's digestive tract. Sometimes biological control can take the form of simply putting up a birdhouse, which will attract wild birds that thrive on insects. Domestic turkeys and chickens can be great at eating insect pests if you can also keep them from eating the crops.

Of course, the whole concept of a pest species versus a beneficial species is a human-created division. We might classify some insects in both categories, such as the minute pirate bugs that bite us in the fall. These tiny insects normally feed on other insects, including corn earworm eggs, a detrimental pest on corn. It is understandable why they appear in our human habitats in the fall after their corn crop habitat is harvested. So, while annoying to us, they are a beneficial insect to the corn crop.

When an ecosystem is balanced, everyone and everything is important. There are no "bad" bugs. There are the wonderful beneficial insects and birds, and then there are their food sources, what we might consider the pests. Farmers and gardeners need to be aware that when they use a pesticide, it can kill not only the pest but the beneficial insects as well. Some level of pest must be present for the beneficial insects to survive. Some insects such as tiny stingless wasps feed on flower nectar but are still beneficial because they lay their eggs in or on the pest, and they devour it upon hatching. These larval stages (think baby bugs that don't necessarily look like their parents) consume the pest. This is one reason that flowers in a garden are an important part of a good biodiversity plan. Even flowering weeds and trees can nourish the beneficial insects, but when farmers began "farming fence-row to fence-row" in the 1970s, habitat for any type of flowering plants was greatly diminished in rural farm areas and likewise the insects that depended on them. Of course, the pests remained as their food sources—the crops—only increased.

The flowers most prized for their nectar by insects generally belong to the Apiaceae family—dill, parsley, coriander, and Queen Anne's lace—and the Asteraceae family: dandelion, sunflower, daisy, coneflowers, and many others. Planting any of these in your garden or at your farm will encourage beneficial insects. At Turtle Farm I put in permanent rows of prairie plants, fruit, herbs, and trees for their blooming food sources. A flower CSA share that I offered some years increased the flower numbers, too.

Most people don't get excited to find a hornworm in their tomatoes, but when I found one in my backyard garden, I was thrilled. This particular tomato hornworm had what looked like little white eggs on its back standing up in multiple rows. That was a sign that *Cotesia congregate,* a tiny, black, stingless braconid wasp less than one-eighth inch long, had visited this worm. It laid eggs in the worm, and they hatched, consumed part of the worm, emerged from the worm's skin, and then spun little cocoons on its back. In a matter of days, they would hatch into new adult wasps. When I found this worm, I knew not to destroy it, or I would destroy the beneficial wasps. Each day I went to the garden and visited the dramatic scenario being played out there. The hornworm never moved from the original location where I found it. It wasn't feeling well and at that point was just a staging vehicle of nourishment for the emerging wasp pupae. Several days later I found its carcass on the ground. All the little cocoon "lids" were off as the new tiny wasps had hatched.

Encouraging the growth of beneficial insects at the farm was sometimes a challenge. I once took a tomato hornworm from the farm and placed it in my garden hoping it would become parasitized there, and then I could transport it back to the farm, spreading the beneficials in the process. That experiment didn't work because I couldn't find the hornworm again. It was too well hidden in "tomato land" or else had been eaten by a bird. Other times, the beneficial wasps at the farm were not so subtle in their work. One year I was lucky to have a stay-at-home mom and recent entomology graduate work at the farm. She was a wealth of knowledge for me. Cathy Hunter and I were seated in the farm stand one day eating our lunches and resting when a large wasp flew by very slowly.

"Look at that wasp," Cathy said. "See that caterpillar it is carrying?" The caterpillar was as big as the wasp.

"It's having trouble maintaining altitude with that big of a load," I said, amazed how it was successfully maneuvering like a helicopter. The wasp made repeated trips during that lunch break with similar prey each time.

"It's got a nest nearby," Cathy said. "It's feeding its babies."

"I think it's just showing us how hard it, too, is working," I replied with a sigh. How could I complain about how tired I was when the insects at the farm were endlessly working to help balance the pest populations?

Insects were constant companions at the farm. In wetter years we were overrun with annoying mosquitoes. Sweat bees loved to land on our sweaty arms to suck the salty liquid. They would not bite if you could resist the tickling and tendency to swat them. Praying mantises were known to transport themselves from one raspberry row to another via the human in the pathway. Many times, as we walked between the crops, grasshoppers would startle and jump away from us, often into a waiting spider's web. We felt like coconspirators in their demise. Webs everywhere would contain golden, green, or brown mummy-like packets of grasshopper meals for the spiders. One day I discovered a pink-wrapped item in a web beneath the raspberries I was picking. This was very unusual. I had yet to see a pink grasshopper, so I looked closer. It turned out to be a web-wrapped red clover blossom. I thought this was a peculiar spider choosing a flower for lunch. On closer inspection, I discovered a tiny bee inside. What a lot of work for few results; the realization caused me to bond immediately with that spider.

One of the insects that was most difficult to control at the farm was the cucumber beetle, either spotted (*Diabrotica undecimpunctata*) or striped (*Acalymma vittatum*). Contrary to what you might think, this little yellow and black beetle does not consume or eat the fruit of the plants, at least at first. Rather, it chews on the newly emerging plant's leaves or stems, weakening them, or chews on more mature plants and infects them with a bacterium that makes them wilt almost overnight. These beetles are hardest on the cucumbers, melons, summer and winter squashes, which are all in the cucurbit family. One reason the population of spotted cucumber beetles was high could be related to the fact that the larval stage of this insect was the Southern corn rootworm. In a state of monocrops of corn and soybeans, it was no wonder this problematic insect (and others such as the bean beetle) was overabundant. Other beetle predators such as birds do not like the bitter taste of the cucumber beetle.

From 2010 through 2012, we cooperated with ISU plant pathologist Mark Gleason for some on-farm research to find solutions for this pest. While one might think of this area of research as the domain of an entomologist, Mark was interested because of the spread of disease by this insect vector. Pest control options we looked at for cucurbits included physical barriers—covering them with a thin polyester fabric for two different lengths of time. Both covered treatments improved yield of the winter squash.

Another option included a later planting date, which took less time and labor and worked best with winter squashes. (A later planting date also worked to reduce damage in green beans from bean beetles.) The solution I found easiest at the farm to reduce labor costs was to do succession plantings of summer squashes and cucumbers. By the time one planting of those crops started to get targeted by and succumb to the beetles, a succeeding crop could be ready for harvest.

Sometimes the abundance of insects got shared with our customers. Ladybugs in particular, *Coccinella septempunctata* (the seven-spotted ladybug), those very familiar beetles that even children recognize, or their less familiar larvae, which look like tiny black and orange alligators, might sleep on the undersides of plants during the night. We harvested crops, especially leafy greens, early in the morning before some insects began to stir. On rare occasions, even with the washing process, a bug might accidentally get packed up and delivered to a home and make a guest appearance in a salad. Cabbage worms that can live in the recesses of broccoli until they morph into cocoons and then butterflies would sometimes make the trip to someone's home. These encounters with wildlife might not be appreciated by some customers, but they made visible the connection with the community of plants and insects that got our food to the table. Pesticides were not being used at Turtle Farm and the food was as fresh as it could be.

I hoped that education about how important insects are to the success of the farm and the growth of nutritious food helped my customers to tolerate the occasional visitor—that bug on their plate. It was further exemplified by our experiences with ladybug larvae, an insect I had never recognized before I started farming. Ladybug larvae often rectified a pest invasion. We found this most noticeable in young okra plants. Farmhand Ben often was the first to notice many pest problems. "Angela, the okra is covered in black aphids," he reported to me one day. "The plants don't look too happy."

I hiked to the okra bed to confirm his sighting. The little black insects practically covered the undersides of the leaves, and the plants were showing signs of being stressed by the sap-sucking aphids. "Do you want me to use something on them?" he asked. Organic farmers are allowed to use certain sprays made from natural ingredients on certain pests.

"Not yet," I replied. "Let's wait a bit longer. This has happened before when the okra was young and just getting established, and I want to see if the beneficials show up to take care of them." Sure enough, a few days later the cavalry had arrived. Ladybug larvae were all over the leaves, making a feast out of their favorite food—aphids! The adult beetles eat aphids as well and most likely had decided the okra buffet would make a good spot for their offspring to hatch. The okra survived and eventually flourished. We had not had to intervene in the natural processes taking place on that crop. The okra arrived on our customers' plates thanks to those ladybugs and their larvae. Once again, the importance of insects to the healthy functioning of a CSA farm never ceases to amaze me.

10

THE HEALING PATH
OF NATURE

You never change things by fighting the existing reality.
To change something, build a new model that makes the
existing model obsolete.
—BUCKMINSTER FULLER

MORE AND MORE SUSTAINABLE FARMERS are working
toward regenerative agriculture with a goal of long-term
health of the land. They are searching for and finding solutions that cooperate with Nature. Regenerative agriculture
promotes soil health and biodiversity, while producing
profitable and nutrient-dense farm products. This kind of
agriculture isn't an individual step applied here and there,
but a system-wide approach to farming. Gabe Brown, a
sustainable, regenerative farmer in North Dakota, has
increased his topsoil two inches in twenty years using
these methods. On his farm, Brown plants diverse cover
crops to build up organic matter and fertility in the soil,
grazes animals on the land to help integrate those crops,
and practices no-till farming to keep the land covered
while cropping. Water infiltrates these soils better and
helps create resilience during drought.

Healthy soil goes a long way toward preventing disease

and pests in crops. I would have loved to have had the kind of success Gabe Brown had with my own soil-building methods. If a disease appeared on the crops at Turtle Farm, I didn't just yank the affected plants out and burn them and believe the problem was solved—an agricultural version of "whack-a-mole." I wanted to know what the soil needed that it wasn't getting that may have caused the problem. What nutritional components were missing that would create a healthy, disease-resistant plant? Were there certain vectors (insects or animals, even the wind) that were spreading the disease, and how could those be mitigated? Perhaps the crops were planted in an area that was too wet or too dry. Maybe the seed that I used wasn't suited to my region. In situations like these I would look for the underlying cause and identify a treatment to avoid problems spreading to the rest of the crop and to protect future crops. A model of prevention on the farm saves a lot in problems later on. The same could be true for human health, as I discovered firsthand in 2007. How many times have you gotten an illness and wondered what might have prevented it? The answer is not always easy to find. Our health care system is more likely to treat the symptoms than find a cause or focus on prevention. I would later be surprised to learn just how little some doctors know about nutrition.

The scene at the farm that October was anything but memorable, but I remember it vividly because of what came after. Ben, Sue, and I were doing the year-end chore of pulling up weed fabric that had been laid in the spring to warm the soils for our sweet potatoes. The fabric created a more tolerable growing environment for the tropical plants. We had harvested the potatoes weeks earlier, but now the season had ended, and the fabric needed to be put away for the winter. One side of the black plastic material had a wooly texture that helped it adhere to the ground. That was great when windstorms tried to yank it loose even when it was stapled in place. But now the weed fabric did not want to release. We strained to pull up, shake out, and fold up the fabric that had gained multiple times its original weight from the added soil. It was nasty, grit-in-your-mouth-face-and-eyes work. Over the seasons, Sue had gained the nickname "Pigpen," after the Peanuts character, and it was never more appropriate than during this chore. I had some sciatica pain in my right leg that made it difficult to pull very hard, probably a result from having pulled too many things too hard that season. At one moment in my frustration as I pulled hard on a stubborn piece of fabric that wouldn't give, I blurted out, "Something's got to change!" Of course, I had in mind some sort of machine that would ease this task for us. Be careful of what you wish for in your future.

Several weeks later the results came over the phone from a nurse. "The biopsy was positive for cancer," she said in a tone that was kind, but matter of fact.

"Okay," I responded. I would process all the ramifications of the breast cancer diagnosis later. My heart sank, but I refused to engage fear and instead began a search for information. "So," I continued, "now what?" That's when my ticket for a train ride through the medical system was punched.

The first stop was surgery, a lumpectomy. I could almost hear the train whistle blowing to announce the next stop. Surgery had automatically set me up with a doctor in radiology. During this process I wondered if I had made the right decision to do radiation. While surgical removal of the lump seemed rational, all I had learned in the sciences was how destructive radiation is to biological systems. I began my own search for more information just as I had for better and more sustainable agricultural practices. I devoured anything that I could find on alternative treatments. I talked with women who had chosen different paths, read books, and checked for alternative healers.

When the five-times-a-week radiation treatments ended after several months, I had a plan. John and I were going to visit our daughter in California, and I asked her to set up an appointment for me with her naturopathic doctor, Gabrielle Francis. Naturopaths weren't allowed to practice in Iowa, but they could in California. I was interested in consulting with someone who could bring in not only the science of traditional medical training but a holistic approach to heal my body. I was curious about the alternative nontoxic therapies that worked with Nature rather than just by attacking a disease. Where were the preventative strategies for my body that paralleled my farming philosophy?

Dr. Francis's office was located in what appeared to be a brownstone residence. I walked up the concrete steps and entered the building. Her waiting room looked like a Moroccan spa with large pillows on the floor under colorful tent-like fabric awnings suspended from the high ceiling and an open sliding glass door leading to an outdoor tropical garden. I was offered tea or a vitamin C drink by a receptionist. When I was summoned to her office, I sat on a love seat across from her. Dr. Gabrielle Francis was a beautiful young woman with black curly hair and a deep olive complexion. In addition to her training as a naturopath, she was an acupuncturist and therapeutic massage therapist. The first question to come out of her mouth was "Are you willing to change?"

"That's why I'm here," I replied. I immediately felt like I had found a mentor. No other doctor had ever asked me to do anything to address my lifestyle, my diet, or my emotional well-being. I was left to fend for myself, so I did. She took a thorough history and ordered hormone tests. Her treatment plan not only offered supplements and dietary guidelines, but lifestyle and environmental changes as well. A world of alternative choices was opened before me to heal and remain healthy. Prevention was a strategy I was very familiar with in my organic farming. Plant better tomato varieties to resist blight. Reduce mildew in squash with better air circulation. Build up the soil for good nutrition. I left Dr. Francis's office that day with enthusiasm and optimism.

The third and final stop on the medical system train ride was a visit with an oncologist. By the time I had returned home from California and met with her, I felt ready to take more responsibility for my health. The oncologist's recommendations were for chemotherapy and hormonal therapy, both with side effects that could reduce my energy level. So far, this medical journey had taken place during the farm's off-season, October to April, and didn't require large energy outputs. I felt fine, but I knew I was headed full blast into a new growing season and would need all the energy I could muster. Proposing chemicals to me, an organic farmer, felt like sacrilege. I decided to step off the train. I was willing to face any consequences of my actions. No further signs of cancer were evident in follow-up tests. With the research I had gathered, I had other alternatives to try that made sense to me. It felt like very serious "on-farm research" with my body as the subject.

Part of the reason many medical doctors do not recom-
mend changes to diet and lifestyle is that they are not
fully educated on the topics, or these treatments are not
approved under their training. I asked my nephew who
was in medical school at the time how much training he
received in nutrition. He said one month. If doctors go into
uncharted territory making unauthorized recommendations, they risk censure or worse from their peers, their
institutions, and insurance companies. But I've found that
more and more doctors and patients are becoming dis-
satisfied with the current health care system. Some are
exploring integrative or functional medicine. The latter
looks at the whole patient for root causes of diseases and
how to treat them just as my naturopath had done. Rather
than pouncing on symptoms with pharmaceutical drugs,
functional medicine seeks causes of those symptoms first
and then determines treatments. This is similar to how I
would tend to my sick plants, the needs of my soil, and my
organic practices on the farm. Sustainable farmers across
the Upper Midwest, many of them finding the conventional
prescribed farming techniques lacking, are also seeking
better growing methods.

I had already rejected the violent metaphor of "fighting" cancer, which I considered a fear-based notion. This
disease was a part in and of me, something that needed to
be understood and redirected to heal. Dr. Francis's model
for healing and prevention included, among other things,
removing sugar, caffeine, and a variety of environmental
toxins such as close contact with cell phones, phthalates
in plastics, and chemical cleaning products. She recommended increasing vitamin D3, omega-3s, iodine, and

DIM (diindolylmethane), a big word for a substance found in vegetables such as broccoli, kale, Brussels sprouts, cabbage, and watercress. I was excited to put this list of preventative and possibly curative tools into practice for my health. The best part was that the garden vegetables and fruits that I grew, the exercise in the fresh air, and sunshine were healing steps right in front of me on the farm.

During all my years of farming I had protected myself with hats and long sleeves for fear of overexposure to the sun. In the process I had become vitamin D deficient, so I began more judicious exposure during my outdoor time. One way I chose to increase my omega-3 levels was to eat not only oily fish like salmon but also grass-fed beef. Researchers are finding that how our animals are raised affects the fat profiles in their meat. The omega-6 to omega-3 ratios recommended by the American Heart Association are 4 to 1 or even lower, and some research has found ratios of 2.5 to 1 have reduced cancer proliferation. The average American diet is closer to a 10–15 to 1 ration of omega-6 to omega-3, which is considered inflammatory. Practical Farmers of Iowa research showed that 100 percent grass-fed beef was able to average a ratio of 2 to 1.

Many people use specific foods as part of an approach for their health dilemmas. Dr. Terry Wahls, a physician with the University of Iowa, relates in her book *The Wahls Protocol* how she used a diet including many vegetables, leafy greens in particular, to help manage her progressive multiple sclerosis (MS). Wahls had been confined to a wheelchair and began researching the connections between mitochondrial and neurological health. (Mitochondria are little energy-producing organelles within our cells.) She eventually returned to walking and is currently working with the National Multiple Sclerosis

Society to investigate the effectiveness of the diet in managing MS. I was heartened by these scientific efforts and began to increase my vegetable consumption, especially those containing DIM, by adding more servings to meals, including breakfast.

Daphne Miller, MD, in her book *Farmacology: What Innovative Family Farming Can Teach Us about Health and Healing*, relates seven visits to farms where she looked for and found connections to our health and how food is grown. One farm used integrated pest management methods, an approach to control pests using a combination of practices that takes the pest's biological information (life cycles), economics, and the environmental hazards for people and property into consideration rather than strictly following conventional guidelines for scheduling applications of pesticides. She also visited with innovative scientists who referred to themselves as "integrative evolutionary cancer researchers." One of these researchers, Bob Gatenby, "turned to agriculture for new ideas on how to approach cancer care." He noted how insects can become resistant to chemical pesticides or genetically modified crops, similar to how cancer cells can turn resistant to chemotherapy. Gatenby declined the "whack-a-mole" method of conventional agriculture and conventional oncology in favor of monitoring a patient's condition to decide what treatments to use that could support the health of that patient yet contain the disease, what he calls "integrative patient management."

As I look back on my health journey, I cannot help but notice the similarities of alternative healing choices to alternative farming practices. Functional medicine strives for developing a healthy body to resist disease, rather than attacking just the symptoms in ways that can compromise the immune system. The same could be said for healthy soils that can be enriched by cover crops and compost rather than synthetic fertilizers such as ammonium nitrate that kill life in the soil. Alternative solutions often take time to take effect. They can require more work and planning. People are often impatient and want quick-acting methods to deal with their disease (think drugs or pills) or their farm fertility and pest problems (think synthetic fertilizers, herbicides, and pesticides).

Some people may be bullied or ridiculed by their doctors or families for trying methods "outside the box." Agriculture "specialists" and other farmers fill that role for the innovative farmers. Medical and farm insurance are tilted toward the traditional models. Many alternative or natural solutions are not covered by health insurance. Some organic farming practices are not fully supported by federal farm insurance programs, and certainly fruit and vegetable crops do not have the federal price supports like the less healthy grains and soybeans. Less and less research is being done to study natural treatments because there is not a lot of money in it. Agricultural companies create genetically modified seeds and then harsh chemicals to kill the resistant super weeds or super bugs resulting from their use. Their answer for the weeds becomes, in addition to glyphosate (Roundup), more toxic chemicals such as 2,4-D and dicamba, with no end in sight for slowing this progression.

Everyone is different and must find their own way to optimal heath and do their own review of the research, which changes practically every day. What I hope to communicate is how important it is for people to take responsibility for their health along with their health care professionals, just as it is important to learn about how their food is grown by farmers and take responsibility in using their food dollars or growing practices wisely.

Eight months after my diagnosis I was at the farm on a June day laying out that dirty weed fabric on the sweet potatoes again. One might think that nothing had changed in that time, but that would be wrong. In my mind there was a world of difference. I gazed at the new crops emerging in the field and saw gifts of healing that I hadn't fully recognized or appreciated before. I had a better grasp on how to take care of myself and trust my decisions for my body and for the farm's soil and crops. My conviction for being in this business of connecting healthy land, food, and people was stronger than ever.

Epilogue
LAND TRANSFER

Knowing that you love the earth changes you, activates you to defend and protect and celebrate. But when you feel that the earth loves you in return, that feeling transforms the relationship from a one-way street into a sacred bond.

—ROBIN WALL KIMMERER, *Braiding Sweetgrass*

DURING GARDEN MEDITATION TIME (think hoeing long rows of strawberries where the cultivator doesn't reach between the plants), when the silences are lengthy and the mind wanders, I would consider what would become of this Iowa farm when my time shepherding it was over. My age had something to do with this conversation in my mind. I was in my late forties when I began this farming endeavor. When we first purchased the property, we thought it would be a temporary commitment to farming, and a good financial investment in land. Turtle Farm was on a state highway across from the town of Granger, so the land price reflected its development potential even then. Little did I think of the love and protective attachment that would come with spending time on that land. It was not a family farm. We didn't even live on the property. It was twenty acres, so its uses to sustain a farmer were limited to high-value crops. Would this island in the midst of farms measuring hundreds or even thousands of acres have any chance of survival after my tenure? Would it be attractive to anyone else as a farm?

Every time I drove to or from the farm, I would become acutely aware of how rapidly good farm ground can get paved over, never to be resurrected again. The cities and suburbs expanded, sucking up the soil and plants around them, turning them into lawns and concrete; it seemed there was little one could do to prevent this sad transformation. Gone was land that could nourish people, plants, and animals in some sort of bad joke idea of progress. Lost! It was an advantage to live close to a metropolitan area to have markets for my produce, but the encroachment of city life also had its destructive disadvantages.

My fantasies during meditation time then became, how do I keep this farm from becoming just another development? How can it remain a farm indefinitely? If it were sold to another farmer, which seemed like a best-case scenario, there would be no protection from it being sold again to a developer in the future. Not making a decision would drop the land in the laps of our children, who might not necessarily make the same choices that were important to John and me. Both of our daughters were establishing lives and families in western states and showed no interest in returning to Iowa.

At some point the idea of cooperative housing entered the conversation. If the farm were owned by a group of people rather than one person, the land would be more protected. Its future would not rest in the hands of a single operator. Exploring this idea led to learning about cohousing, a type of collaborative housing that began in Europe. Residents in this type of neighborhood actively participate in the design and operation of their own community.

Private homes contain all the features of conventional homes, but residents have access to common facilities, such as open space (the farm!), gardens, playgrounds, and a common house. The common house features shared-use facilities such as a large kitchen and dining area, laundry, workshop, libraries, guest rooms, or whatever needs the community deems important to that group of home-owners. The shared facilities enable a reduction in size of the individual homes. Most cohousing developments use green approaches to building and living. I could see how this would be a protective solution for continuing to operate the farm as a farm. The housing could fit on the top five acres of the property, which had the least productive soil and the best view, leaving the remaining fifteen acres, owned in common by all the households, for continued cultivation.

In 2007 I introduced the idea of cohousing to the Turtle Farm CSA members. An interested group gathered to pursue it and formed the Turtle Farm Cohousing Community. Our mission was "to preserve Turtle Farm by creating a model of a diverse, sustainable, cohousing community." We received tentative support from the city of Granger and Polk County. A member of the Granger City Council commented that the idea seemed to connect to Granger's past when Granger Homesteads were created for the miners' families. We invited Charles Durrett, a national leader in the development of cohousing, to speak in Des Moines. People from Iowa City who were also considering a cohousing project came to hear him speak.

Many elements of this type of living resonated with my customers and others who learned about it. I was looking forward to it as a retirement residence. But when it came time for a financial commitment, most interested parties assessed what they valued in their current communities: close proximity to friends, grocery, movies, library, and doctors. The farm location twenty miles out of town would be a bigger adjustment than most of them wanted. Perhaps a better marketer, a more astute developer, or an angel investor could have made a difference. I only know that after several years of trying to spark enough interest in this idea of cohousing and not getting viable numbers, we let that flame flicker and die.

It was back to square one; cohousing wasn't going to work. Around this time Practical Farmers of Iowa (PFI) began noting how land transfers of farms were occurring more frequently and decided to commission a play, *Map of My Kingdom,* which began performances in 2014, to explore this topic. The author was Mary Swander, retired English professor at Iowa State University and former poet laureate of Iowa. Her play illustrated the complications in family dynamics that can result from farmland transfers. John and I wanted to be able to prevent these problems by making the decisions ourselves. One of our concerns was eminent domain seizure of property. One could not totally rule that out, but there was plenty of property around Granger with development potential, so we felt that possibility was minimal unless the Iowa Department of Transportation decided to expand the existing two-lane highway on the west side of the property. That risk would exist regardless of who owned the farm.

An idea that showed promise was to donate the farm to a nonprofit. For many farmers, the land we farm is a huge investment. Paying off the mortgage is like making deposits into a retirement fund. The land becomes a source of our wealth. By 2010 I had managed to pay off the farm from my profits. To turn over that total investment to a non-profit was not something John and I felt we could afford to do. However, our experience considering cohousing had led us to understand that the top five acres of land could be separated from the rest of the farm without harming the potential for its continued use. Selling part of the farm would offset our investment losses as would the charitable donation. We decided to put those five acres of land up for sale. Plan B was born. By this time, I had retired from active farming, and we had been renting the land to Ben, my employee who had been most interested in a farming career, for three years. We had no timeline or need to rush this sale and were willing to wait to get the price we felt we needed to enable the donation.

It wasn't long before a phone call came inquiring about the land. "Hi, my name is Sue Harney. My husband and I have bought the land to the east and north of your farm. We were wondering if you would consider being annexed into the city of Granger? We can't leave an island of property when we get annexed in," she said.

I wasn't aware who had bought those properties or that they would need my property to be annexed into Granger before they could be developed. But I did know that the development to the south of the farm had officially become part of the town. "Well, the top five acres of my property are for sale. If that sells, I would consider the annexation," I informed her.

"What are you asking for the property?" she inquired.

When I told her the price, she was taken aback. "Oh, we couldn't afford that," she said. "We paid much less for the surrounding properties." They had bought the thirty-seven acres to the north and the forty acres to the east.

"That's fine," I said. "We aren't in any hurry to sell it."

Only a few weeks later, the realtor representing Sue and her husband was talking to our realtor. They were willing to raise their offer if we would sell seven acres instead of just five. We hated to lose the extra two acres of farm ground, especially since about half the asparagus patch was on it. After discussing the possible changes coming to the farm with Ben, we eventually compromised and agreed to include the extra two acres when they met our minimum price.

In the meantime, we had been talking to various nonprofits that seemed appropriate caretakers for the remaining thirteen acres. The list included the Iowa Natural Heritage Foundation (INHS), the Community Foundation of Greater Des Moines, Sustainable Iowa Land Transfer (SILT), and PFI. INHS and SILT needed a fee to be paid in addition to the donation for management expenses. The Community Foundation had a minimum value of a property that it would accept (which Turtle Farm didn't meet), and there was no promise that the property might not be sold to access its value for the organization's needs. INHS would have limits on development but no insistence that the property be farmed. Only PFI and SILT could confirm that they would see that the farm remained a farm.

At the time, PFI had had other land donations, but none had been fulfilled yet. They were dependent on the deaths of the donors. These donations would meet part of their mission statement of helping beginning farmers by leasing the land to them. Land access—finding land at a reasonable price—can be one of the hardest things to obtain for beginning farmers who are short on capital, especially if they have not inherited a farm. I was privileged to have my husband's job to guarantee a loan for our farm. I would not have qualified otherwise.

PFI was where my heart was because of my history with the organization. I called executive director Sally Worley to see if they wanted our land donation. Sally asked for information on the farm expenditures that might be beyond the scope of the renter, such as the well, barn, and driveway maintenance. Things PFI had to consider in the case of Turtle Farm included the income potential from the lease of thirteen acres and if that would cover the costs of upkeep and personnel. She asked about the current lease arrangement with Ben. I requested that Ben be allowed to remain on the farm the first year so that he could adjust to his new landlords and build a relationship with them for any future years. He also would need some adjustment to the reduced size of the farm and loss of income from the disruption of the asparagus patch.

PFI and their lawyer considered the ramifications of owning a farm in the city limits. Every city has rules and regulations on everything from weeds to noise. Some utility right of ways might disrupt farming activities during development of the surrounding area. After careful consideration, the PFI board voted to accept our gift. Turtle Farm would be the first test case of land management for them. Plan B became a reality. We worked diligently with PFI to finalize the donation just before the end of the year for a reduction in our taxes on the land sale. The sale and donation of the property brought the farm ownership full circle from twenty years earlier. I was no longer the caretaker for those special twenty acres. It was a bittersweet feeling. It felt good to know that the land would be taken care of and remain a farm. But I had an identity crisis as a retired farmer without any land—like a parent without a child.

I would miss the cycles of creation that I got to influence each year producing a new crop to share with my customers. I would miss trying to get it right, which could be euphoric the few times it happened, and stressful when it didn't. Wendell Berry expresses some of my feelings toward farming in *Bringing It to the Table: On Farming and Food*. "Why do farmers farm, given their economic adversities on top of the many frustrations and difficulties normal to farming? And always the answer is: 'Love. They must do it for love.' Farmers farm for the love of farming. They love to watch and nurture the growth of plants. They love to live in the presence of animals. They love to work outdoors. They love the weather, maybe even when it is making them miserable. . . . They love the measure of independence that farm life can still provide. I have an idea that a lot of farmers have gone to a lot of trouble merely to be self-employed to live at least a part of their lives without a boss."

It was a joy to grow a wider variety of vegetables on the farm than I could squeeze into my backyard garden no matter how much lawn was dug up. Would my garden meet my needs to get my hands in the soil? To hedge my bets on that, it was written in the sale agreement with PFI that I could use a small plot of land at the farm for my own vegetable production as long as I wanted. That helped my withdrawal. Then I got chickens.

"Chick, chick, chick!" I call out to the young hens. They rush from their coop through bent welded-wire channels that meander through the garden beds and orchard. I feed them Japanese beetles that I collect off the raspberries and peaches. These are my tiny chicken tractors that weed and feed the garden, eat grubs and insects, and stir the soil. When they have cleared one bed, I move the portable chunnel pieces to another. If the beds are in full production, then they get to patrol the pathways. I've found that they love kale and collards more than my human customers did. The chickens add to my postfarming contentment. But when the annual USDA surveys arrive at the end of the year asking if I am a landowner or actively farming, I can no longer check the box.

This land may have been turned over to someone else's care, but the feelings of love, respect, and gratitude remain in my heart not only for Turtle Farm but for land everywhere that sustains all life. I would contend that anyone who has farmed or gardened looks at the soil with a different perspective than those who haven't—with expectations of its potential, its enduring resilience, its life, its gifts.

Wise farmers learn that they also need to give back to help sustain the land. But are we not all stewards of this Earth? Others can also find a connection and a sense of thanksgiving. Danielle Wirth fostered that connection when she brought her students to the farm. CSAs foster it when their customers make an intentional choice about how their food is grown. Volunteers at our Iowa food co-op are a part of it, too. There are many ways for everyone to nurture our Earth.

To express a mindful gratitude to the Earth and its bounty, Robin Wall Kimmerer in her book *Braiding Sweetgrass: Indigenous Wisdom, Scientific Knowledge and the Teachings of Plants* beautifully relates an Indigenous Haudenosaunee address of thanksgiving, known as "Greetings and Thanks to the Natural World": "Today we have gathered and when we look upon the faces around us we see that the cycles of life continue. We have been given the duty to live in balance and harmony with each other and all living things. So now let us bring our minds together as one as we give greetings and thanks to each other as People. Now our minds are one." The address continues with an inventory of thanks to all the natural world from plants to water to fish to sun.

From the moment I step out of my house and fill my lungs with fresh air each morning, I savor this natural world that I am a part of. I feel the responsibility of my residence here. I am grateful for the journey I have had stewarding a piece of land regardless of its size—a twenty-acre farm, a backyard garden, a houseplant. There is no limit to how I can continue that stewardship in new and various ways.

May you find your ways to do so also.

Part II
Harvest

ENJOYING FAVORITES—
AND CHALLENGES—
IN YOUR CSA BOX

. . . so much beauty passes through your hands—*of form,
and color, and texture.* And energy too. . . . Each grain of
rice, each leaf of kale, charged with life and the power
to nourish. It's heady, feeling yourself a kind of conduit
for the life force!

—LAUREL ROBERTSON, *The New Laurel's Kitchen*

AND NOW THE REAL REASON for all the fuss. The food! What
we choose to eat is very personal. It is rooted in the foods
we were fed by our parents and the food culture that we
grew up in, the biases we choose to believe in from adver-
tising, and, of course, taste. It is very hard to convince people to change their eating habits unless they want to. My
assumption was that when people joined my CSA, they
wanted to expand their food horizons. Their personal likes
and dislikes varied to an extent that I was not prepared for.
Making all my customers happy with the vegetables that I
grew was not a task that I could ever fully accomplish. I
tried to accommodate their many opinions when I could.

I asked my customers in year-end surveys which crops
they would like to drop and which crops they would like
to add. The surveys exposed their love–hate relationships
with food. Swiss chard, eggplant, beets, and okra were

the most polarizing vegetables in my CSA. I encouraged them to try new recipes because often people have only tried something prepared one way, and that has colored their perspective. If they thought okra was "slimy," I gave them ideas for roasted or pickled okra. If they had suffered through canned beets in their youth, I challenged them to try them roasted and cut up into salads. Once a customer, Lisa Croyle, and one of her daughters came to pick up their CSA box at the farm, and we got into a fun discussion of food rules at their house. Maybe it will work with people at your house. Lisa offered, "At our house you're only allowed to have one food that you don't eat. Liking your food is optional, eating it isn't."

I would have put canned spinach in that category as the one food I didn't eat as a child. I vividly remember one time giving up a coveted dessert because I could not stomach the limp greens in order to clear my plate. Mother rarely served it. My father chose not to grow spinach because in the South the weather can turn hot so quickly the plant would have bolted. Come to think of it, my father didn't grow any greens. Perhaps he didn't have the time or inclination to want to pick them. The season for greens would have been late winter when the homegrown pickers were in school. I think fresh spinach would have been so far superior in taste that whether we ate it fresh or cooked, it would have made all the difference. One green we did eat was poke greens. As a teenager I would find it along our dirt roads. Why I liked this green and not cooked spinach is beyond me. In their raw form, the greens are considered poisonous; they require brief simmering and then pouring off the cooking water before continued cooking. We served them with vinegar so that overshadowed the actual taste of the greens, but they looked like spinach.

When I was farming full-time, I would not get home before 5:30 and sometimes as late as 7:00 p.m. I was the cook in the family and obviously a big proponent of this wonderful, fresh food. I was bound and determined that I would prepare it, regardless of how tired I was. I found myself adapting recipes to simpler versions that took less time. That's something all working people can appreciate. I learned how to play with my food. To that end, I have included some tips in the recipes that follow. Some of these recipes may not be fancy or intricate, but they still taste great. The simpler the preparation, the more opportunity for the freshness and flavor of the vegetables to stand out. And the recipes here are certainly not exhaustive. They are a sampling of what I or my customers prepare and enjoy. I hope you do, too. Here are the crops and recipes meant to entice you to try them in new ways and make some new friends, presented the way Nature intended. It's called cooking with the seasons.

Crops are listed by the month they might first appear in the Upper Midwest in your CSA box (though they might appear in multiple months). The use of protected growing tunnels or greenhouses by farmers might alter this list. Check your local CSAs for the food choices they make. You might be surprised at how much they can differ, especially since some CSAs have branched out to include eggs, flowers, dairy, breads, and meats.

When a recipe calls for vegetable oil for cooking, I like to use extra-virgin olive oil, coconut oil, or ghee from grass-fed dairy. Choose the oils that you prefer. Sometimes recipes call for a range of ingredient amounts. You can adjust those to your liking.

THE APRIL CSA BOX

Asparagus

Green Garlic

Nettles, Wild Dandelions, and Garlic Mustard

Asparagus

Asparagus generates a lot of excitement as one of the first vegetables of the season. In April we would often encounter our first sightings of snakes in the asparagus patch, sunning their cold-blooded bodies in the straw mulch. That made the search a dual experience. One eye out for asparagus spears, one eye out for our snake friends.

I like my first few servings of asparagus simply steamed and buttered. My taste buds seek to reconnect purely to this amazing and unique vegetable. But after that, I like to prepare this creative recipe sent in from one of my CSA customers. Mark McAndrews says, "These are all strong flavors that tend to complement and compete with each other in this dish (which is why I give no amounts). The bitterness of the arugula and the funk of the blue cheese can dominate easily, so use a light hand with those two ingredients—adjust the amounts you use to fit your own tastes."

Mark's Asparagus on Pasta

Asparagus, trimmed, cut into 1-inch pieces
Olive or other oil
Walnut halves
Arugula, washed, coarsely chopped
Blue cheese (such as Maytag), crumbled
Penne pasta, cooked and drained

Sauté asparagus in oil until just starting to brown on one side, about 5 minutes. Toss a handful of walnut pieces into the skillet and continue cooking for another 2 minutes. Turn off the heat, add arugula and blue cheese. Cover with lid until the cheese melts; the heat remaining in the pan will wilt the arugula and melt the cheese. Toss with cooked, drained penne pasta. (Recipe sent by Mark McAndrews, adapted from Cooksillustrated.com.)

Asparagus and Quinoa Salad

Dandelion greens, sorrel, and lemon balm arrive in the same season as asparagus and can be lively additions to this salad.

1 pound fresh asparagus, trimmed and cut into 1.5-inch pieces
    (about 2 cups)
1 tablespoon olive oil
½ to ¾ cup cooked quinoa
1 cup artichoke hearts, quartered
Lemon vinaigrette (see below)
½ cup chives, coarsely chopped (or diced red onion)
½ cup fresh lemon balm or sorrel, coarsely chopped (optional)
½ to 1 cup young dandelion greens, coarsely chopped (optional)
Salt and pepper to taste

Preheat oven to 400 degrees. Toss the asparagus and olive oil in a small bowl. Place asparagus on a baking sheet. Roast for 15–20 minutes, turning halfway through, and watching carefully that it doesn't burn. Remove from oven and set aside to cool. While asparagus is roasting, cook quinoa according to package directions in a small saucepan. Once done, stir and set aside to cool. Place artichoke hearts into a medium serving bowl. Make vinaigrette (see below) and toss well with the artichoke hearts in the serving bowl. Once cooled, add asparagus and quinoa to the serving bowl. Add chives (or onions), herbs, and dandelion greens if desired. Toss well. Season with salt and pepper. Serves 2–4.

   LEMON VINAIGRETTE: Make Basic French Vinaigrette (page 146), substituting 2 tablespoons lemon juice for red wine vinegar and increasing olive oil to 6 tablespoons.

Asparagus Soup

If it's near the end of asparagus season, and you find an opportunity to get extra, blanch and freeze it for a winter soup treat.

1 pound fresh asparagus
1 tablespoon ghee or oil
1 shallot, minced
1 clove garlic, grated
2–3 cups chicken broth
1 small yellow potato, peeled
½ cup cream or nut milk, such as almond or macadamia
Salt and white pepper to taste

Wash and trim the asparagus, snapping or cutting off the woody ends and cutting into 1-inch pieces. In a medium pot, heat the ghee and sauté the shallots about 3 minutes, then add the garlic. Cook 30 seconds, then add the chicken broth and bring to a boil. Meanwhile, cut up the peeled potato into ½-inch dice. Add potato and asparagus to boiling broth and cook until potato is tender, about 5–8 minutes. Add cream or nut milk. With an immersion blender or food processor, purée the soup until smooth. Adjust seasoning with salt and pepper. Gently heat and serve. Serves 2–3.

Green Garlic (also called Fresh Garlic)

While the main garlic harvest comes in July in the Upper Midwest, green garlic can arrive even before the scallions, which many of my customers mistakenly took them for. (Garlic has strap-like leaves, while scallions have round, tubular leaves.) Green garlic is milder than its mature bulb state. Some garlic was grown specifically for this early harvest, but sometimes if I looked in the previous year's garlic bed, some green garlic would magically appear from escaped bulbs there. Green garlic arrives just in time to use in salad dressings on greenhouse lettuces or to store in the refrigerator and save for the early lettuce greens from the field in May. It is a primary ingredient in this homemade French vinaigrette. When the bulb garlic arrives later, use it instead.

Basic French Vinaigrette

2–3 green garlic stalks, white parts minced or 1 garlic clove, minced
¼ teaspoon salt (kosher preferred)
½ teaspoon Dijon mustard
2 tablespoons red wine vinegar
2–4 tablespoons olive oil
Salt and pepper to taste

Put the garlic and salt in a small bowl or mortar. Using the back of a spoon or a pestle, crush the garlic against the salt. Add the mustard and vinegar and whisk till well mixed. Add the olive oil to your salad greens and toss (by hand, or with salad tongs if you don't want to get dirty). Add the vinegar mixture and toss again. Check for seasoning. These amounts can be varied according to your taste.

Nettles and Other Wild Things

Sometimes Nature's bounty surrounds us and nurtures us with little effort if we would but take notice. When the farm crew and I recognized this wild green pantry, we offered these healthy items to our customers. Nettles, purslane, and lamb's-quarter were abundant and tasty. Dandelion challenged us to try it raw or cooked. Residents of other countries could even find uses for more of our "weeds." In one instance a couple from Japan filled a large tub with red root pigweed that they took home and prepared. It is an edible green, but one that I have not explored. I was just happy they were pulling a lot of our weeds. Unfortunately, we never found takers for some of the most noxious weeds—Canada thistle and foxtail. Some foragers say you can eat parts of both, but this is not common, to my knowledge.

Among the first green shoots of the season, perennial nettles would grow along the tree line. These are an excellent green for a spring tonic. Use gloves and pruners or scissors to cut the upper 8–12 inches of the plant and place in a bag or bucket. Once in the kitchen, continue to wear gloves as you pluck or snip the leaves from the stem, which can be tough, and place into a colander. Sauté the greens with garlic and butter. Once cooked, the nettles will no longer sting. They also make a nice tea with a clean, grassy taste. Put a small (gloved!) handful into a cup of boiling water. Steep for 5 minutes and pour through a strainer. Enjoy!

Another plant that the farm crew nibbled on while weeding was lamb's-quarter. A relative of spinach, it has a tangy richness to its tender young leaves. Lamb's-quarter makes a zesty addition to salads or, best yet, a snack directly in the field.

Dandelion greens emerge early, too. Pick these bitter greens when young and before flowering for the most tender and desirable flavor. Use them raw in salads (see Asparagus and Quinoa Salad, page 144) or cooked like other greens. They are usually combined with other ingredients to balance out their astringent taste. The flower petals are edible, too, and not as bitter. Obviously avoid any dandelions that may have had applications of pesticides.

A relatively new noxious weed in the Upper Midwest and many other places is garlic mustard. The seeds of this plant were brought from Europe, and it is overtaking many woods in the Eastern and Midwestern United States and the wildflowers that live there. Its rounded, almost kidney-shaped leaves are best eaten young before they turn bitter and taste similar to mustard with garlic overtones. If you're going to be pulling it anyway, try making a pesto from the younger plants or leaves and serve with crackers (see Pesto, page 191).

Wild Spring Salad

Dandelion greens
Sorrel
Chives
Sprouts
Other greens as desired
Green garlic
Vinaigrette
Salt and pepper to taste

Use what wild foods you can find, augmenting them with tamer vegetables such as lettuce or spinach that may be available. Make a vinaigrette with the green garlic (see Basic French Vinaigrette recipe, page 146) leaving out the mustard and using balsamic vinegar instead of red wine vinegar. Its sweetness counters the bitter flavor of the wild foods. Toss and adjust seasoning.

THE MAY CSA BOX

Arugula

Bok Choy

Cilantro

Greens

Kale

Kohlrabi

Lettuces

Mustard Greens

Radishes

Spinach

Spring Turnips

The spring CSA boxes of mid-May to mid-June started out lightweight with crops of spinach, arugula, radishes, lettuces with edible pansies, and more asparagus. Soon they were joined by sugar snap peas, kohlrabi, kale, broccoli, herbs, garlic scapes (the flower of the garlic), scallions, and strawberries. Some crops—lettuces, strawberries, and radishes among others—had multiple varieties that we shared. Only a trained tongue like mine could probably distinguish between a 'Northeaster' and a 'Jewel' strawberry, but some crops like radishes were more varied in character between the mellow 'French Breakfast', 'Pink Beauty', and 'Cherry Belle' versus the spicier 'Plum Purple' so that most customers could tell the difference.

Arugula

Arugula adds a peppery flavor to fresh lettuce salads and sandwiches, but it also works well as a cooked green. See Greens (page 153) and Mark's Asparagus on Pasta (page 143).

Bok Choy

I try to eat one or more servings from the healthy brassica family every day. Bok choy, kale, arugula, collards, and broccoli do not keep as well as the storage cabbage, kohlrabi, or radishes, and should be eaten as soon as possible.

Like me, most of my customers did not grow up eating bok choy. It took just one great recipe for it to become a regular at our house. You can use four small bok choy such as the 'Mei Qing' variety or a larger one such as the robust 'Joi Choi'.

Mushrooms and Bok Choy with Asian Sauce

8–12 ounces mushrooms, cleaned, trimmed, sliced (can use shitake, baby bellas, or button)
2 tablespoons coconut or olive oil
1 medium bok choy or 6 baby, trimmed, stalks chopped, green leaves separated, sliced
2 cloves garlic, minced
1-inch ginger piece, minced
1 cup vegetable or chicken broth
1 tablespoon corn starch
2 tablespoons soy sauce
1 tablespoon fish sauce
½ to 1 teaspoon toasted sesame oil
1 cup basmati rice, cooked

In a large skillet sauté mushrooms in heated oil over medium heat, about 3 minutes. Add bok choy stalks, garlic, and ginger and sauté 2 minutes more. Then add bok choy leaves and sauté another minute. Add broth and bring to a simmer and cook for 2–5 minutes. The bok choy stalks should be tender-crisp.

Meanwhile put corn starch in a small bowl. Add 1 table-spoon water and stir. Add soy sauce and fish sauce to starch mixture. Add to skillet and stir until the broth thickens and becomes clear. Remove from heat and add sesame oil. Stir well. Serve over rice. Serves 2–4.

TIP: Other vegetables such as broccoli, sugar snap peas, or snow peas can be used instead of or in addition to bok choy. (Adapted from *Bon Appétit*, February 2007.)

Bok Choy with Coconut Pineapple Sauce

1 medium head bok choy, greens and stems separated
1 tablespoon coconut oil
2 cloves garlic, minced
1-inch piece of ginger root, minced or grated
1 13-ounce can coconut milk
½ cup crushed pineapple
2 tablespoons lime juice
½ teaspoon salt
¼ teaspoon curry powder
⅛ teaspoon red pepper flakes
Cooked rice

Cut the bok choy stems into 1-inch chunks. Coarsely chop the greens. Heat the oil in a large skillet over medium heat. Add in the bok choy stems and sauté for several minutes, turning frequently. Place the bok choy greens in the skillet with the stems and continue to cook, stirring often until greens have wilted nicely. Add garlic and ginger root and cook for another minute. Add remaining ingredients (except rice) to a medium bowl and whisk briefly. Pour over the bok choy and heat through. Season to taste and serve with or over rice. Serves 2–4.

NOTE: To make this a heartier main dish, use a pound of ground turkey seasoned with ½ teaspoon salt to shape into 1-inch meatballs. Prepare the sauce ahead of time and simmer the meatballs in the sauce for about 20 minutes until done. Then sauté bok choy as above and pour meat sauce over it before serving. Swiss chard or spinach can be substituted for the bok choy.

Cilantro

Cilantro is one of the first herbs to sprout in the spring. Once hot days come it can quickly bolt, so take advantage of its spicy, bright goodness quickly. If it should flower and make seeds, you now have coriander, which you can also save for cooking. Cilantro is added last in dishes because it tends to lose its flavor with cooking. As a dried herb, it is not nearly as flavorful as fresh, so I preserve it by making a pesto variation using just the herb and olive oil (see Pesto, page 191). Freeze for later use.

Greens

Spinach, Swiss chard, kale, collards, and other greens are often cooked in a similar way with just the cooking times adjusted. Start by heating a teaspoon of oil or ghee in a skillet over medium heat, adding in a thinly sliced garlic clove to sauté for 30 seconds. Then add the chopped green of choice, ¼ cup water or broth, cover, and steam until done. This takes only a few minutes for spinach, slightly longer for chard, and longer yet for kale and collards. Watch to see that it doesn't cook dry. After the green is tender, you can add in other options such as butter or red pepper flakes if desired, even cooked bacon. Season to taste with salt and pepper.

Kale

Smooth leaf kale, lacinato or dinosaur kale with leathery leaves, and the curled varieties such as 'Winterbor' are the main types of kale. You may find different types at different times of the year. We started off in the spring with 'Red Russian', which is only slightly curled and a bit milder than the other kales, which take longer to mature. All kales stand up well to cooking in soups or baked with other vegetables.

Parmesan Kale Salad with Raisins

1 large bunch of kale, washed, destemmed, and torn into pieces
½ cup raisins or currants
1 lemon, zest removed and saved, then juiced
½ cup grated Parmesan cheese
3 tablespoons olive oil
½ cup toasted nuts such as pine nuts or walnuts (coarsely chopped)
Salt to taste

Put kale pieces in food processor and pulse until finely chopped. Remove kale to medium bowl and add raisins or currants, lemon juice, and zest. Toss. Stir in Parmesan, olive oil, and nuts. Toss again. Season to taste. Serves 2–4. (Adapted from eat-drink-smile.com.)

Salmon Soup with Kale

½ cup quinoa
2 tablespoons oil or ghee, divided
8 ounces mushrooms, cleaned and sliced (shitake, baby bella, button, or maitake)
1 onion, coarsely chopped
5 cups chicken or vegetable broth (homemade is best)
1 bunch kale, destemmed and chopped (about 2 cups), or spinach
1 pound salmon (or cod), bones removed
Pinch of red pepper flakes (optional)
Salt and pepper to taste

In a small saucepan, cook quinoa in 1 cup of broth or water according to package directions. Meanwhile, heat 1 tablespoon oil or ghee in a skillet over medium high heat. Add mushrooms and sauté until the moisture from the mushrooms is gone and they lightly brown. Remove from skillet and set aside. Add the second tablespoon of oil or ghee to a soup pot and heat over medium heat. Add the onion and sauté until translucent. Add the chicken broth and heat to boil. Add the kale and allow to cook for about 5 minutes. Then add the cooked mushrooms. Add the salmon fillet and pepper flakes. Simmer for approximately 5 minutes until salmon is cooked through. Remove salmon fillet from the broth, remove skin, break into bite-size chunks, and return to the broth. Adjust seasoning to taste. Serves 4. (Adapted from Food.com.)

Kohlrabi

This "sputnik" vegetable in the cabbage family is always fun on a food quiz. Many people don't know what it is or how to use it. It forms a bulb that is actually a swollen stem, and its leaves emerge from there. It's slightly cabbage-like flavor can be grated into a slaw, eaten raw after peeling, or roasted. Even the leaves can be used as a green. 'Azur Star' kohlrabi is a purple variety, but once peeled, it is green inside. If you have an abundance, you can peel, boil, and mash them like potatoes.

Angela's Marinated Kohlrabi

2 small or 1 medium kohlrabi
2 tablespoons rice wine vinegar
½ teaspoon sugar (optional)
1–2 drops toasted sesame seed oil
1 teaspoon minced spring garlic or green onion
¼ teaspoon salt
2 teaspoons olive oil

Peel and thinly slice the kohlrabi into half-moons. Mix
the remaining ingredients well and pour marinade over
the kohlrabi in a glass container, tossing to mix well. Chill.
Serve cold or at room temperature. Serves 4 as an appetizer.

Lettuces

There are so many heirloom lettuces that it is difficult to
try them all. Running a CSA gave me an excuse to try growing numerous varieties. One lettuce called 'Cracoviensis'
is so temperamental that it bolts at the first sign of heat,
so it was always the first in line for the season and just
as quickly gone. (If you want to grow a lettuce for summer's heat, look for Batavian types.) Sometimes a lettuce
has multiple names such as 'Freckles', 'Forellenschluss',
'Speckled Trout', and 'Trout Back', all a lovely rust-speckled
romaine lettuce. 'Deer Tongue' lettuce is my favorite—an
heirloom buttercrunch, an apt description for its buttery
taste and crunchy leaves. You won't find it in any grocery
store as it's very fragile and is difficult to harvest and wash
without breaking outer leaves, leaving it looking a little mangled on a good day. But it still tastes so good! One
tip for harvesting is to cut the lettuce and let it sit for five

minutes to just begin "relaxing" or wilting before collecting it for washing. This reduces the breakage of the crisp
outer leaves.

One of the first recipes I shared with my CSA customers was for a salad dressing that my mother-in-law, Elsie
Tedesco, taught me. Like many people, I had grown up
on bottled dressing and was unfamiliar with simple oil
and vinegar mixtures. She tossed the salad first by hand
with the oil, then added the vinegar and seasonings and
tossed again. The method lends itself so nicely to changing the vinegars and oils to make a multitude of different
dressings. Elsie mainly used cider vinegar and corn oil. I
have progressed a little further on the homemade dressing scale and enjoy a French vinaigrette. These homemade
dressings are so flavorful, take little time to prepare, and
don't have all the additives of many bottled dressings or
the less desirable soybean or canola oil. There are two
secrets to a good salad. One is *dry* greens, and the other is
the *hand massage*.

Elsie Tedesco's Salad Dressing

Bowl of favorite greens, washed and dried (use salad spinner or
  towel dry)
Onions, cucumbers, peppers, tomatoes, etc.
2 tablespoons olive oil
Salt and pepper (kosher salt and freshly ground pepper preferred)
2–3 tablespoons herbal, wine, balsamic, raspberry, or other
  favorite vinegar

Drizzle the oil over the greens with any other additions that
you want, such as onions, cucumbers, etc. With clean hands,
gently toss/massage the salad greens until they are well

coated with the oil. Sprinkle with salt and pepper. Drizzle
the vinegar of choice over the greens. Toss with tongs this
time. Serve immediately.

∿ The following two lettuce recipes may seem out of
the ordinary, but they can help broaden our preconceived
notions that lettuce is just for salads. They are both great
ways to use up excess lettuce or mixed greens that may be
past their prime or if you are just overloaded with lettuce in
your spring CSA boxes.

Sautéed Mushrooms and Lettuce on Pasta

8 ounces penne pasta
1–2 tablespoons olive oil or ghee
8 ounces mushrooms, cleaned and sliced (shitake or baby bellas
   are my favorites)
2 cloves garlic, thinly sliced
⅛–¼ teaspoon red pepper flakes
¼ cup white cooking wine
¼ cup grated Parmesan
2 small or 1 large head romaine lettuce in 1-inch slices (other lettuce
   could be used)
Salt and pepper to taste
Optional add-ins: cooked peas, crisp bacon bits, halved cherry
   tomatoes, prosciutto

Cook penne pasta in boiling water until done and drain.
Meanwhile, heat oil in a large skillet and sauté mushrooms
until browned. Add in garlic and red pepper flakes for the
last few minutes of cooking. Add wine and reduce liquid.
Add cooked pasta, Parmesan, lettuce, salt and pepper, and
any optional add-ins. Turn off heat and stir until well mixed.
Serves 2–4.

Lettuce Pesto

2 garlic cloves
Approximately 3 cups lettuce or mixed greens, coarsely chopped
¼ cup pine nuts (or walnuts)
¼ cup Parmesan, grated
¼ cup olive oil
¼ teaspoon red pepper flakes (optional)
Salt and pepper to taste

Place garlic cloves in a food processor until chopped. Add remaining ingredients and process again until the lettuce is incorporated, but still has texture. Serve as a dip on crackers, over cooked pasta, or as a sandwich spread. Makes approximately 1 cup.

Mustard Greens

See Greens, page 153.

Radishes

At Turtle Farm, I grew 'French Breakfast' (red with white tips), 'Champion' and 'Cherry Belle' (both red), 'Pink Beauty', 'Plum Purple', and 'White Icicle' radishes, which range from mild to spicier respectively. The hotter the weather, the more zing in the radish.

No one enjoyed their vegetables with more drama than customer Bonnie Boal. She delighted in each and every one. Bonnie also hosted a weekly pickup site for the CSA boxes and would often have a delicious, prepared appetizer set out nearby with chairs to encourage people to linger. She had a real gift for combining food and community.

Radish and Cabbage Coleslaw

Bonnie says, "I made *fabulous* coleslaw with half cabbage, half radishes (every kind you gave me), a little mayonnaise, some sherry vinegar and kosher salt and freshly grated black pepper. I imagine it would also be good with just radishes. The rest of the radishes I cut from the greens (which I cooked, chopped, and froze for winter happiness!) and put in the refrigerator in a container of water. That keeps the radishes from drying out, and they are cold, crunchy, and delicious when I get the munchies. There is a small dish of kosher salt right next to the refrigerator door!" (Recipe from Bonnie Boal.)

Spinach

Spinach is wonderful in everything from lasagna and ravioli to soups and salads. See Greens, page 153, and Salmon Soup with Kale, page 154. Spring spinach makes a nice seasonal salad with sliced strawberries. Add sliced red onions, goat or feta cheese, roasted walnuts or pecans, and balsamic or poppy seed dressing. For a hearty spinach dish try this chickpea stew.

Chickpea and Spinach Stew

1 tablespoon olive oil
1 medium onion, finely chopped
2 large garlic cloves, minced
¼ teaspoon red pepper flakes
1 tablespoon fresh rosemary, minced
2 tablespoons chopped parsley
2 large tomatoes, peeled and diced, or 1 28-ounce can diced
    tomatoes
2 15-ounce cans chickpeas, rinsed
2 bunches spinach, stems removed, coarsely chopped
Salt and pepper
Aioli or garlic mayonnaise (see below)

In a large skillet sauté the onion in the olive oil. Add the
garlic, red pepper flakes, and rosemary and sauté several
minutes longer until the onion is soft. Add the parsley,
tomatoes, and chickpeas and simmer covered for 15 minutes. Add in the spinach, stir well, and taste to see if salt is
needed. Cook several minutes until spinach is tender. Add
pepper as desired. Serve in bowls with a spoonful of aioli.
Serves 4. (Adapted from *Vegetarian Cooking for Everyone*, by
Madison, 1997.)

To make aioli, add 4 large, minced garlic cloves and
a pinch of salt to a mortar and crush with a pestle until
a paste forms. Transfer to a small bowl. Add ½ teaspoon
lemon juice, 1 cup mayonnaise, and salt to taste.

Soused Spinach

*The most unusual and elegant spinach dish I have eaten was
at a friend's home—a Japanese ohitashi or dashi-marinated
spinach shaped into a delightful two-by-two-by-two-inch green
cube. While kombu seaweed and bonito flakes may not be
common staples in your kitchen, they are easy to find, and
it can be fun and worthwhile to explore this simple dish.*

1¼ cup dashi (see recipe below)
1 bunch young spinach
Pinch salt
½ teaspoon sugar
1 tablespoon tamari soy sauce
Bonito flakes for garnish (optional)

To make dashi, place a 4x2-inch piece of kombu in 4 cups of
water to soak for several hours if possible. Heat liquid in a
saucepan just to the boiling point and remove the kombu.
Add ⅓ cup bonito flakes, bring the water to a boil, then turn
off the heat and leave for 5 minutes. Strain.

Boil a large pot of water and add the spinach leaves for
about 30 seconds. Remove and drain the spinach in a colander, then quickly cool the leaves by dunking in cold water.
Drain again and squeeze out all water. Form into a round or
square log about 4 inches long. A sushi rolling mat is helpful
here if you have one. Slice spinach into 2-inch sections. Set
aside.

Add salt, sugar, and soy sauce to the dashi. Place spinach
sections in a glass container. Pour dashi mixture over, cover,
and refrigerate 5–6 hours. Serve at room temperature with
a sprinkle of bonito flakes. Serves 2–4. (Adapted from *Japanese Cooking: A Simple Art,* by Shizuo Tsuji, 1980.)

Spring Turnips

Early spring turnips that newcomers may mistake for white radishes are not strong-flavored like their fall turnip cousins. They are yummy raw, tasting a bit like a mild radish. Cooking brings out a mild turnip flavor. At Turtle Farm, I grew the 'Hakurei' variety.

Ground Lamb with Turnips and Greens

1 tablespoon oil such as ghee or olive oil
1 large onion, chopped
1 pound of ground lamb, grass-fed preferably
1–2 cloves garlic, minced
4 carrots, ½-inch sliced
2 tablespoons fresh rosemary, chopped
¼–½ cup water
6 'Hakurei' or other spring turnips, ¾-inch chunks, with greens,
    ribs removed and roughly chopped, separated (or in the fall,
    substitute daikon radish, ¾-inch chunks without greens)
2 tablespoons fresh parsley, chopped
Salt and pepper to taste

Heat the oil in a large skillet over medium heat. Add the onion and sauté until translucent (about 5 minutes). Add the ground lamb and stir to break up into crumbles. After the lamb loses all its pinkness and begins to brown, remove from heat and remove any accumulated fat in the pan. Return to the heat and add the garlic to sauté with the lamb for another minute. Add the carrots and rosemary leaves. Stir well and add water, cover, and cook for 5 minutes. Add turnips, stir, and cover to cook until the turnips and carrots are tender. Add turnip leaves and parsley, stir, and cover to cook 2 more minutes or until greens are wilted and just tender. Season with salt and pepper to taste. Serves 4.

   TIP: Arugula or kale, chopped, could be used instead of turnip greens.

THE JUNE CSA BOX

Broccoli

Cabbage

Cucumbers

Garlic Scapes

Peas

Raspberries

Scallions

Strawberries

Summer Squash

Swiss Chard

Broccoli

This simple recipe was fashioned after a soup I ate on a trip to Oregon for a horticultural meeting. The lightly browned broccoli and onion add an umami richness to the flavor of the soup.

Sautéed *Broccoli* and *Onion* Soup

2 tablespoons ghee or olive oil
1 head of broccoli, cut into small florets
1 medium onion, chopped
2 cups chicken broth
Salt and pepper
Parmesan cheese, grated

Heat oil in large skillet. Add broccoli and onion. Sauté until the vegetables are starting to brown slightly. Add in chicken broth and bring to a boil. Simmer for about 5 minutes or until the broccoli is just barely tender. Season to taste with salt and pepper. Serve with Parmesan cheese. Serves 2–4.

Cabbage

Simply cooked in a small amount of broth or sautéed with onion in a skillet are easy ways to include more of this healthy, hearty vegetable in your diet. I always include cabbage in chicken soup. It pairs deliciously with bacon.

Roasted Cabbage with Bacon

1 head green cabbage
Oil of your choice
Salt and pepper
8 ounces sliced bacon, medium or thinly sliced

Heat oven to 400 degrees. Cut cabbage into slices approximately ½-inch thick, keeping each section intact. Lay
sections on a large baking sheet and drizzle lightly with
oil. Sprinkle with salt and pepper. Cut bacon into as many
pieces as you have sections of cabbage and lay over or wrap
the cabbage pieces with them.
    Roast for about 20–30 minutes until bacon begins to
crisp, watching that cabbage edges do not get too brown.
Serve immediately. Serves 4. (Adapted from thekitchn.com.)

∿ Red cabbage, while slightly stronger in flavor, has a
healthier nutrient profile than its green sibling—more
vitamins, flavonoids, and antioxidants. Since it is often
ready in the fall when apples are ripe, they make a delicious
combination.

Red Cabbage with Apples and Sausage

2 tablespoons cooking oil
1 medium onion, diced
½ to 1 medium head red cabbage, quartered, cored, and finely sliced
2 cooking apples, cored and sliced
8 ounces sausages, cooked and cut into 1-inch pieces
Salt and pepper

Heat the oil in a large skillet. Add the onion. Stir for a few
minutes until the onion is translucent. Add the cabbage.

Season with 1 teaspoon salt. Cover and cook slowly until the cabbage is very tender, stirring occasionally, about 10 minutes. Add in the apples and sausages and cook about 10 minutes longer. Season to taste. Serves 4. (Adapted from *Vegetarian Cooking for Everyone,* by Madison, 1997.)

Cucumbers

My husband John's favorite cucumber recipe is simply sliced cucumber and onions marinated in vinegar-water (1:1 ratio or your preference) with salt and pepper added. During one robust harvest year, we served them with hummus, put them in smoothies, and even froze them in chunks for use in smoothies or dips throughout the winter.

Cucumber, Onion, and Tomato Salad

*I once prepared lunch for a northern European guest
of my horticulture advisor, Gail Nonnecke. In the midst
of a fancy quiche, bread, and dessert, he was most excited
about this simple salad. "It reminds me of home," he said.*

1 medium cucumber, halved lengthwise and sliced into
  ½-inch half-moons (peeling optional)
1 medium to large sweet onion, peeled, quartered, ¼-inch sliced
2 medium tomatoes, peeled and cut into eighths
2 tablespoons olive oil
2 tablespoons tarragon vinegar
Salt and pepper

Combine cucumber, onion, and tomatoes. Toss with olive oil. Add vinegar, salt, and pepper and toss again. Serves 2–4.

Garlic Scapes

A useful and somewhat overlooked part of the garlic plant is the flower stalk or scape. These arise on stiff-neck garlic about a month before the bulbs are mature. We would remove these so that the full energy of the plant could be directed to the bulb formation. Garlic scapes can be grilled, cooked to flavor dishes, added to a flower bouquet, or used to make garlic pesto (see Pesto, page 191). When my last garlic bulb has been used in the winter, I turn to my frozen garlic scape pesto to extend the season until the first green garlic is ready in May.

Peas

Here's another vegetable that needs little help and many times is best eaten raw, especially if you are trying to get children to like them. Snow peas or sugar snaps in stir fries, salads, or with dips need no recipes. If you should inconceivably grow weary of these methods of preparation, here's a soup recipe that I rely on often. I use shelled peas for this, but snow peas and sugar snaps could be used as well.

Minted Pea Soup with Harissa

1 tablespoon olive oil
1 small onion, diced
1 large carrot, diced
3 cups peas, shelled, fresh or frozen
4 cups vegetable or chicken broth
2 tablespoons fresh mint, minced

2 tablespoons fresh lemon juice
Salt and pepper to taste
Harissa oil

Heat olive oil in a soup pot over medium heat. Add onion and carrot and sauté for 5 minutes. Add peas and broth and bring to a boil, simmering just until the peas and carrots are done, approximately 5 minutes. Add mint and simmer 5 minutes more. Add lemon juice and remove from heat. Place vegetables in a food processor or use a hand blender to purée the soup, being careful of the hot liquid. Adjust seasoning to taste. Serve immediately by spooning into bowls and drizzling ½–1 teaspoon harissa oil on each bowl of soup. Serves 2–4. (Adapted from food52.com.)

Raspberries

Raspberries would seem to be easier to pick than strawberries; after all, the plants are much taller. However, if one does not lean over and look up through the canes, you may be missing half the harvest. This up and down yoga makes raspberry picking more strenuous than at first glance. The most prolific red everbearing variety that I grew was 'Autumn Brittany', but I preferred the slightly sweeter flavor of 'Autumn Bliss'. 'Jewel' black raspberries were harder to grow, but I favored their complex, dark flavor even more. Several of my customers would hand their CSA pint of raspberries to their children for entertainment on the ride home, never getting a taste for themselves.

Little embellishment is needed here. I often make a raspberry sauce for use on desserts. This is easily done by cooking 1 quart of berries with ¼ cup water. When the berries have simmered for a short time, put them through a food mill to remove the seeds. Further reduce the sauce with more cooking as desired. It may be sweetened with stevia, sugar, or honey to your taste. It is especially good over ice cream or with anything chocolate.

Scallions

Scallions were the first onion crop I planted in the greenhouse, transplanted to the farm, and harvested in the spring. Slice not only the white stems into salads but also the green leaves. Or leave whole to use with dips or roast with other vegetables, being careful that they don't overcook. 'Evergreen Hardy' was the variety I used for Turtle Farm, but some CSA growers would use winter or "walking" onions that overwinter and are ready to harvest even sooner. I now use these in my home garden.

Strawberries

Adorning a perfect jewel seems superfluous. A strawberry straight out of the patch cannot be improved on, in my humble opinion—not with sugar, or cream, or chocolate. My tongue would eventually become sore from all the extra vitamin C that I was consuming while picking strawberries, a result of eating "defective" berries. 'Earliglow' and 'Jewel' were two favorite varieties. The former was not as productive but is the standard for flavor. The latter is larger, more productive, and holds its berries higher off the ground, and the berries are firm enough to stand up to handling while still tasting delicious. Be sure to freeze any extras to put in smoothies during the winter.

Turtle Farm Strawberry Shortcake

Drop Biscuits

2¾ cups flour, chilled
2 tablespoons plus 2 teaspoons sugar
1½ tablespoons baking powder
7 tablespoons unsalted butter, chilled
2 cups heavy cream, plus extra for brushing on biscuits
1 teaspoon salt

Sift dry ingredients. Cut butter into flour mixture. Add heavy cream and mix gently until ingredients have just come together. Don't overwork. Divide into 8 or more pieces and drop onto sheet pan lined with parchment. Brush with cream. Bake 25–30 minutes in oven preheated to 375 degrees.

Berries

4 pints Iowa organic, vine-ripened strawberries
Sugar and lemon to taste

Cut 3 pints of berries and mix with sugar and lemon. Let stand for 1–2 hours to release juices. Do not refrigerate. Just before serving, slice remaining berries (also at room temperature) and mix with other berries.

Vanilla Whipped Cream

½ quart heavy cream
1 teaspoon vanilla
2–4 tablespoons vanilla sugar (sugar stored with a whole vanilla bean to impart flavor)

Whip cream adding vanilla and sugar to taste. Whip to soft peaks.

ASSEMBLY: Cut cooled biscuits in half with serrated knife. Place bottom half on individual serving plate. Spoon berries and juice over bottom half, add whipped cream. Dip or drizzle cut side of top half of biscuit in juice and place on top of berries and cream. Add more berries and a dollop of whipped cream. Finish with the most beautiful whole, stemmed berry. Serves 8 generously, 12 sensibly. (From Stephanie Lock, daughter of farm members Joyce and Fred Lock.)

Summer Squash

Simply sautéed summer squash is the dish we enjoy the most, whether we are using green zucchini, yellow, or the wonderful, tasty heirloom 'Costata' squash. The most unusual and a favorite squash for me is 'Zucchetta Rampicante' or 'Tromboncino', an Italian heirloom with firm texture and a mild squash flavor. We often saw it growing in the backyard gardens of Italian homes on our visits there. It's best planted on a trellis so that its vining stems can climb, and the almost two-foot fruit can hang down straight. Otherwise, growing on the ground they tend to curve like the letter "C" or a fishhook.

Sautéed Summer Squash

1 tablespoon ghee or oil
3 small or 2 medium summer squash, halved lengthwise and then
    sliced into half-moons
1 medium onion, halved and sliced into ¼-inch half-moons
Favorite sausage, cooked (optional)
Parmesan cheese, grated (optional for topping)

Heat ghee or oil over medium heat in large skillet on stove. Add summer squash and onion. Cook covered, stirring occasionally, for 5 minutes. Partially remove lid and continue to cook until squash and onion are lightly browned and cooked through. Add sausage if using and cook until heated through. Remove from skillet and serve immediately. Pass the Parmesan. Serves 2–4.

Grilled Lamb Shish Kebab with Summer Vegetables

Marinade

1 pound boneless leg or shoulder of lamb, trimmed to 2-inch cubes
Salt and pepper
1 tablespoon chopped fresh rosemary
2–3 cloves minced garlic
¼ cup olive oil
1 tablespoon lemon juice

Vegetables (vary depending on availability)

2 tablespoons olive oil
1 large sweet onion, sliced into 8 wedges with some stem attached
    to hold together
1 zucchini squash, cut into ¾-inch diagonal slices
2–3 small sunburst squash, quartered
1 large green pepper, cut into 8 strips
1 small yellow pepper, cut into large strips
2–3 medium tomatoes, peeled and quartered
6 ounces feta cheese, crumbled

Couscous

10-ounce box of couscous
Pita bread

Season trimmed lamb with salt and pepper. Combine rosemary, garlic, ¼ cup olive oil, and lemon juice in a glass dish. Add lamb and marinate covered for at least 1–2 hours. Prepare charcoal and place lamb on skewers.

In large sauté skillet, heat oil over high heat and add onion. When onion starts to brown, add squash and peppers. Continue to sauté on high heat. Do not overcook. Vegetables should be browned and a little crunchy.

Meanwhile, start grilling lamb to medium rare and prepare couscous according to package directions. Add tomatoes to vegetables and blend gently. Crumble feta cheese over top of vegetable mixture, cover, and turn off heat. Place couscous on individual dinner plates, arrange vegetables and lamb on top. Serve with pita bread. Serves 2–4. (From Turtle Farm member Joyce Lock.)

Zucchini Delight

One of my employees brought this recipe to my attention.
My husband John likes it despite the fact that it has no onions.

1 cup mozzarella cheese, grated or ¼-inch cubes, divided
1 28-ounce can tomatoes, chopped or diced, drained (reserve juice
    to cook the lentils in)
3 small or 2 medium zucchinis, chopped
1 teaspoon dried oregano
2 tablespoons basil pesto or ½ cup chopped fresh basil
¼ teaspoon red pepper flakes (½ teaspoon if you are more
    adventurous)
2 cups cooked lentils
2 cups cooked basmati rice

Preheat oven to 350 degrees. In a large casserole dish, combine half the cheese with the tomatoes, zucchini, oregano, basil, red pepper flakes, lentils, and rice. Stir together. Top with remaining cheese. Bake uncovered for 45 minutes. Let rest 5 minutes before serving. Serves 4. (Adapted from *How It All Vegan*, by Tanya Barnard and Sarah Kramer, 1999.)

Zucchini Mounds

*Long ago our family gave up tacos in the hard shells because
of the dripping, crumbling mess they would become. Instead,
we would take a handful of corn chips, crumble them onto
our plates, and add the toppings. It was far less messy eaten
this way with a fork. Here's another deconstructed recipe
that a customer sent me to try.*

2 tablespoons pine nuts
1–2 tablespoons oil
1 medium zucchini, chopped into ½-inch dice
1 small red or yellow bell pepper, finely chopped
1 small onion, thinly sliced
2 garlic cloves, minced
1 teaspoon ground cumin
¼–½ cup fresh cilantro, chopped
¼ teaspoon salt
Ground pepper
Corn chips
Lime (optional)
Your favorite salsa
2 cups Monterey Jack cheese, shredded

Toast the pine nuts in a skillet being careful not to burn.
Heat the oil in a skillet over medium heat. Add the zucchini,
pepper, onion, garlic, and cumin. Lightly sauté until the
veggies are soft. Add the cilantro, salt, and pepper. Serve
over crushed corn chips. Add a squeeze of lime if desired.
Top with salsa and cheese. Serves 2–4. (Adapted from *Simply
Organic*, by Jesse Ziff Cool, 2008.)

Swiss Chard (see also Greens)

Whether you use the many colors of 'Bright Lights' Swiss
chard or the sturdier, green 'Fordhook Giant', the largest
leaves work best for this recipe.

Swiss Chard Rolls
with Walnuts and Salsa

8–10 large Swiss chard leaves
1½ cups walnuts
2 teaspoons tamari soy sauce
2 teaspoons olive oil
1 teaspoon ground cumin
½ teaspoon garlic powder
1 teaspoon paprika (or pinch cayenne)
Salt to taste
1 cup salsa
Pinch smoked paprika

Fill a large skillet halfway with water and bring to a boil.
Meanwhile, carefully trim large stems from Swiss chard
leaves and stack the leaf halves together. Taking half the
leaf halves, place in boiling water for 1–2 minutes. Carefully
remove with a large spatula, keeping the leaf halves from
tearing. Place in a colander to drain, then set on a plate to
cool slightly. Cook the remaining half of the chard in the
same manner.

In a food processor, chop the walnuts into meal. Add next
five ingredients and process again. Taste for seasoning.

Remove chard leaves from the stack carefully one at a
time, place 1 tablespoon walnut filling on one end and roll
up the leaf. Continue with the remaining leaves and arrange
on a serving plate. Add the smoked paprika to the salsa and
heat gently in a small saucepan. Spoon some of the salsa
over the stuffed leaves. Serve remaining salsa alongside.
Serves 2–4. (Adapted from vogueandvegetables.com.)

THE JULY CSA BOX

Beans (Green)

Beets

Carrots

Collards

Garlic

Onions

Potatoes

Purslane

In mid- to late summer, the CSA boxes grew heavier with a bounty of produce: potatoes, onions, garlic, cucumbers, summer squash, eggplant, peppers, raspberries, and tomatoes. Beets, cabbage, green beans, okra (for those brave enough to try it), and bouquets of basil made appearances, too. It became obvious at this point how I had been tempted in January to select so many varieties of vegetables. Yellow tomatoes ('Nebraska Wedding', 'Garden Peach'), pink tomatoes ('Brandywine', 'Arkansas Traveler'), green tomatoes ('Green Zebra', 'Evergreen'), and yes, red tomatoes, whether paste, roma, or slicers, were all represented. Why grow just one potato variety when there were those with white flesh, yellow flesh, or purple flesh. Irresistible fingerling potatoes were small in size but made up for it in flavor. Varieties can be so unique that I was shocked when I asked at a farmer's market once what variety of potato the grower was selling, and the farmer did not know! Perhaps it was because I came from the kitchen as a cook first and then to the farm as a producer that this smorgasbord of choices meant so much to me.

Green Beans

Some of my customers over the years have made requests for certain crops to be grown. Gourmet cook Joyce Lock once requested *haricots verts*—the small French green beans. I was resistant because the farm crew gets weary picking green beans. The thought of picking enough tiny ones to deliver to my customers made me recoil in horror. However, I was assured by other vegetable growers that *haricots verts* are prolific enough and easy enough to pick that the work isn't so bad. This turned out to be true for the most part. 'Maxibel' was our reliable workhorse for the *haricots verts*. 'Jade' was my favorite for regular green beans.

Restaurants can be inspiring for recipe creation. On a wonderful trip to France, we ate at Restaurant Rech in Paris where I ordered a *haricots verts* salad. It was an amazing discovery with pine nuts and grated Parmesan cheese sprinkled over the top. I was so enamored that I ordered it again when we returned to the same restaurant the following night. Huge disappointment! A different chef must have been working—no pine nuts, no Parmesan. The salad was lackluster and boring. What a difference a few careful touches and ingredients can make. When I returned home, I created this recipe to approximate the first delicious salad. Don't leave out the pine nuts or Parmesan cheese!

Roasted French Green Bean Salad with Pine Nuts and Parmesan

1 pound *haricots verts* (thin French green beans), trimmed, washed, and dried
3 tablespoons olive oil, divided
2 cloves garlic, minced
Salt and pepper to taste
2 tablespoons red wine vinegar
¼ cup pine nuts
¼ cup Parmesan cheese, grated

Heat oven to 400 degrees. Toss beans with 1 tablespoon olive oil. Spread in single layer on a baking sheet; roast on top shelf in oven about 20 minutes, stirring halfway through cooking time. Meanwhile, mash garlic with ½ teaspoon salt; add vinegar. Whisk in remaining 2 tablespoons olive oil. →

When beans are done roasting, remove them from the oven and reduce oven to 350 degrees. Toss beans and dressing in a bowl; season with salt (if necessary) and pepper. Spread pine nuts on baking sheet. Roast them, shaking pan occasionally and watching closely, until lightly browned (1–3 minutes). Sprinkle pine nuts and Parmesan over tossed salad. Serve warm or at room temperature. It may be made with regular green beans (roast them a little longer), and with sliced sautéed mushrooms instead of pine nuts. It can also be made by steaming or boiling the green beans, draining and drying them well before adding the dressing; this saves time, but the roasting sweetens them nicely. Makes 4–6 servings.

Green Bean and Potato Salad

A friend brought this dish to a potluck, and I've enjoyed it ever since. Everyone seems to enjoy the horseradish seasoning.

1 pound green beans, trimmed and snapped
2 pounds potatoes, washed, peeled, cut into ¾-inch pieces
Salt and pepper to taste

Dressing

1 cup mayonnaise
2 eggs, hard boiled, peeled and chopped
1 tablespoon horseradish sauce
1 teaspoon lemon juice, or to taste
1 teaspoon soy sauce or coconut aminos
1 tablespoon minced garlic

Cook green beans in boiling salted water until just tender. Drain. Set aside. Meanwhile, cook potatoes in just enough boiling water to cover until tender. Drain. Put into a large bowl and add the green beans. Make dressing by mixing remaining ingredients together. Add to potatoes and beans and stir to mix well. Adjust seasoning. Serve immediately or refrigerate for serving later. Serves 4.

Beets

Farm employees Ben, Sue, and I had a friendly rivalry about certain vegetables. Take beets, for instance. Ben and Sue think they smell like "dirt" when they are cooking. (Most farmers would prefer the term "soil.") I think beets are fun to try multiple ways. There are probably more of you who feel like Ben and Sue, but give this recipe a try. Or perhaps you would like some milder beet varieties such as 'Three Root Grex' or 'Golden' beets. Beets pair easily with citrus or other fruits and some kind of allium, such as garlic or onions. Feel free to substitute any of those in this or other beet recipes.

Beets and Oranges (or Peaches) with Raspberry Vinaigrette

1 pound small to medium beets, scrubbed
1–2 oranges or peaches
2 cloves garlic, minced
½ teaspoon salt
2 tablespoons raspberry vinegar
3 tablespoons olive oil
1 teaspoon grated gingerroot (optional)

Heat oven to 350 degrees. Place beets (in their skins) in a baking dish and cover with lid or foil. Roast beets until tender, about 40–60 minutes, depending on their size. When cool enough to handle, peel, slice thinly, and place in a bowl. Peel the oranges (or peaches) and divide in half. Place flat sides down on cutting board and slice each into about 4 half moons. Remove and discard seeds if any from orange slices. Add to beets. Make a vinaigrette out of the remaining ingredients: mash garlic with the salt, add vinegar, and whisk in olive oil. Stir in grated gingerroot, if using. Toss with beets and oranges. You can serve this immediately, but it's best if allowed to chill and mellow. Makes 2–4 servings.

Shredded Beets and Orange with Balsamic Vinegar

If you want to cook a beet dish (or any other firm vegetable) quickly, try cutting it in smaller pieces or grating it first. This dish comes together in a jiffy.

2 tablespoons oil, olive or coconut
3 small or 2 medium beets, grated
Salt
1 tablespoon balsamic vinegar
1 orange, zested and juiced

Heat oil in a large skillet over medium heat. Add grated beets and pinch of salt and cook, covered, about 5 minutes. Stir often. Add vinegar, cover and cook another minute. Remove skillet from heat and add orange zest and juice. Mix well and serve warm or at room temperature.

VARIATION: Use ⅓ cup dried or frozen fruit of choice, such as cherries, cranberries, raisins, raspberries, or blueberries, instead of the orange. (Adapted from lehighvalleylive.com.)

Carrots

Every year I went through a precise ritual regarding carrots: I plant a nice bed of carrots in May, I run to tend other crops, the carrots emerge slowly, the weeds emerge quickly, the carrots get lost among the weeds. Each July I call my friend and carrot-growing guru Gary Guthrie, a.k.a. the Carrot King, to see if I can get some of his carrots. He introduced me to 'Bolero' carrots. You know if you've been successful in educating the public about their food when a vegetable becomes known by its variety name. At a dinner with friends, the wife, who was a gourmet cook, proudly brought in the final side dish of the meal, proclaiming "and these are the 'Boleros.'" 'Boleros' are a delicious, sweet fall carrot.

Carrot Salad with Lemon Vinaigrette

The French like to serve a simple grated carrot salad with a lemon vinaigrette dressing, which is a fast, lively way to serve this humble vegetable.

3–4 large carrots, grated
1–2 tablespoons shallot, minced (or green onion)
1 tablespoon parsley, chopped
2–4 tablespoons fresh lemon juice
½ teaspoon Dijon mustard
2 tablespoons olive oil
Salt and pepper to taste

Place vegetables in a medium bowl. Make the vinaigrette with the remaining ingredients. Add to vegetables and toss well. Serves 4.

Carrot and Bean Quesadilla with Curry and Cumin

This recipe uses cooked carrots and takes a little more time,
but makes enough for leftovers that heat up easily.

2 cups sliced carrots
½ cup chopped onion
4 tablespoons olive oil, divided
2 cloves garlic, minced
2 teaspoons curry powder
1 teaspoon ground cumin
½ can white or black beans, drained and rinsed
½ teaspoon salt, as needed
½ cup chopped cilantro
Flour tortillas
4 ounces mozzarella cheese, grated or thinly sliced
Oil
Salsa

In a saucepan cook carrots in a small amount of water until tender. In a skillet, sauté onions in half the olive oil, then add garlic, curry, and cumin at the end. Purée the carrots with the remaining olive oil (and a small amount of the carrot cooking water if needed) in a food processor. Add the sautéed vegetables, beans, salt, and cilantro and process again. Mixture should be thick enough to hold its shape. Put 3–4 tablespoons purée on one side of a tortilla. Add a small amount of cheese and fold over the tortilla. Lightly brown each side of the folded tortilla in oil until heated through and golden and cheese is melted. Serve with salsa on the side. Serves 2–4.

Collards

See Greens, page 153.

⌐▭▭▭▭▭▭¬

Garlic

Garlic harvest is an activity when we encouraged volunteers to help us in the field. Hanging the bulbs to dry in the barn is very aromatic. One volunteer claimed that the smell cured her cold. We grew both soft-neck and stiff-neck varieties, such as 'Inchelium' and 'German Extra Hardy' respectively. The latter had such large cloves, it was puzzling to decide how many of them to use in a recipe calling for a clove of garlic. Do not sauté your garlic in oil too long as once it browns it can turn bitter.

Finger Lickin' Edamame with Garlic Sauce

This glaze was inspired by a soybean appetizer served to us in a San Francisco bar. If a dish haunts you after eating it, you can always try to recreate it at home.

1 pound edamame (soybeans), in the shell, rinsed
2 tablespoons soy sauce
1 teaspoon roasted sesame oil
1 tablespoon vegetable oil
1 tablespoon rice vinegar
2 garlic cloves, minced or grated
1 teaspoon brown sugar or honey
2 tablespoons sesame seeds
Kosher salt

Boil edamame in salted water 5–8 minutes. Drain and place in bowl. Combine other ingredients except salt in a sauce-pan and bring to a simmer, stirring, just long enough to dissolve sugar or honey. Pour over hot edamame and toss with kosher salt to taste. Serve immediately, letting diners squeeze the beans out of the pod into their mouths. Have napkins handy. The recipe works with shelled edamame, too, better eaten with a fork. Makes 6–8 servings.

Lamb with Garlic and Rosemary

2 pounds lamb stew meat (or a small leg of lamb)
4 garlic cloves, halved lengthwise
2 or 3 sprigs rosemary, 8 inches long
1 cup red wine
Salt and pepper

Preheat oven to 225 degrees. Place the lamb in a covered baking dish. Put the garlic and rosemary among the chunks of lamb (or in the case of a leg of lamb, make slits to insert the garlic and lay the rosemary under and on top of the leg). Add the wine. Salt and pepper the lamb. Cook for 5–6 hours, checking late in the cooking time to see if some of the liquid needs to be replenished with some water. Remove rosemary sprigs. Serves 4–6. (Adapted from *Smith and Hawken: Gardeners' Community Cookbook,* by Victoria Wise, 1999.)

Onions

There is little cooking in our house that does not start with onion. I'm sure my husband would say it's his favorite vegetable. One of the fun things about starting onions from seed for the farm is that there are lots of choices to try. Two favorites are 'Ailsa Craig' and 'Red Long of Tropea', both early sweet onions. One of the not so fun things about growing onions is how susceptible they are to weed pressures. Many crops can shade out competition when they get to a certain size, but not the skinny, tall leaves of the onion family. In addition to a simple Cucumber, Onion, and Tomato Salad (page 167) you can make good use of summer onions in this tart.

Onion Tart

2 large sweet onions, thinly sliced
2 tablespoons oil
Salt and black pepper to taste
1 12-inch pie crust (optional)
2 cups shredded Gruyère cheese
½ cup basil leaves
2 large tomatoes, sliced
4 eggs, beaten
2 tablespoons grated Parmesan cheese

Preheat oven to 375 degrees. Toss the onion slices with the oil and season with salt and black pepper. Arrange the onions on the bottom of a glass 9-inch pie plate (and crust, if using). Spread the cheese on top of the onions. Layer the basil leaves on top of the cheese. Arrange the tomato slices on top and add in eggs. Sprinkle with Parmesan. Bake for 45 minutes to 1 hour, or until the crust is golden brown and a knife inserted halfway to center comes out clean. Cool slightly before slicing. Serves 2–4. (Adapted from foodnetwork.com.)

Potatoes

Potatoes come in many different varieties. Most people are familiar with the dry, mealy russets that are the familiar fluffy baked or French fried potato that mashes well but can disintegrate in a soup. I grew white potatoes ('Red Chieftain' and 'Caribe') that are versatile mashed or in soups (see Green Bean and Potato Salad, page 180, and Leek Potato Soup, page 201); waxy potatoes such as 'Carola' and 'Yukon Gold' that are best in soups or roasted; colored potatoes ('All Blue') that often are the texture of russets; and fingerling potatoes that are small, finger-shaped, waxy potatoes. Fingerlings were also the most challenging to harvest, which is why I like 'French Fingerling', the largest of this type of potato, better than 'Russian Banana', 'Bintje', and 'La Ratte', which are small and easy to miss at harvest, but their flavor can't be beat, especially roasted. Thank goodness their thin skins don't need peeling—that would be a hand-cramping task.

Roasted Fingerling Potatoes

1 tablespoon olive oil
2 cloves garlic, sliced
2 pounds fingerling potatoes, scrubbed and sliced lengthwise
2 tablespoons herbs of choice (thyme, rosemary, sage), chopped
½ teaspoon kosher salt
¼ teaspoon fresh ground pepper

Preheat oven to 400 degrees. Place olive oil in a small skillet and gently cook garlic for several minutes to flavor the oil. Remove the garlic and set aside. Put the potatoes in a bowl and toss with the flavored olive oil when cooled. Put parchment paper on a cookie sheet and add the potatoes. Roast in the oven for 15 minutes. Remove from the oven and sprinkle herbs and garlic slices over the potatoes. Return to the oven for an additional 10 minutes or until tender. Remove potatoes, sprinkle with salt and pepper. Serves 4.

Purslane

Purslane is an annual but persistent resident that is considered a weed. It is a warm-weather succulent plant, an uninvited guest in most gardens, that Artemis Simopoulos, MD, discovered is the richest source of omega-3 fatty acids of any green leafy vegetable yet examined. It can be used raw in salads or lightly cooked in stir-fries. I give preference to the fleshy leaves that are best picked when young. Although I find its flavor a bit bland, that makes it easy to add to many dishes. In the remote chance that purslane is not in your garden, some seed companies now sell the seeds of this newly discovered superfood.

THE AUGUST CSA BOX

Basil

Eggplant

Okra

Peppers

Tomatoes

Basil

Be sure to make plenty of pesto during the summer when basil is at its peak. Freeze portions in small containers or ice-cube trays and place in plastic bags in the freezer so that you can make dishes like pizza, pasta sauce, or others during the winter when you might have more time. At times I grew lemon, lime, Thai, cinnamon, and holy basil for teas or cooked dishes.

Pesto

2 large cloves garlic
2–4 tablespoons pine nuts (or walnuts)
2 tablespoons Parmesan cheese, grated
3 cups firmly packed fresh basil leaves
¾ cup olive oil
¼ teaspoon salt

Add all ingredients to a food processor and grind just until all the basil is incorporated, but before it is the consistency of baby food. Add more olive oil to create the thickness you desire.

VARIATION: Make the pesto with just the basil and olive oil for any uses when you might want the fresh herb flavor, but you don't need the nuts or Parmesan added. Freeze these for later use, but be sure to label correctly so you know which pesto version you are storing if you make both kinds.

Thai Chicken with Basil

½ ancho chili pepper, finely chopped
2 tablespoons soy sauce
1 teaspoon apple cider vinegar
2–3 tablespoons basil pesto
2 tablespoons ghee or coconut oil
1 large onion, halved and sliced ¼-inch thick
1 small chicken, cut up (or 4–6 pieces thighs and drumsticks)
1 tablespoon cornstarch
Salt and pepper to taste
Brown or white rice, prepared

Mix the chili pepper, soy sauce, vinegar, and pesto. Set aside. Heat the oil in a large skillet and add onions. Sauté briefly. Add chicken pieces and lightly brown on each side.

Add chili mixture over the chicken and stir to mix. Cover and cook over lowest heat setting until chicken is done, approximately 30 minutes. Uncover. Add 2 tablespoons water to the cornstarch and stir to mix. Add to pan juices and stir until it thickens. Adjust seasoning. Serve over rice. Serves 4. (Adapted from *Recipes from a Kitchen Garden,* by Renee Shepherd and Fran Raboff, 1994.)

Lemon Basil Tea

½ cup lemon basil leaves
2 cups boiling water
Stevia or honey (optional)

Pour boiling water over the lemon basil leaves. Allow to steep for 10–15 minutes. Strain into a cup. Sweeten with stevia or honey as desired. Serves 2.

Eggplant

John's favorite eggplant recipe is simple. Eggplants are naturally "thirsty" so I prefer to brush them with oil and then broil them rather than pan fry to reduce oil absorption.

Angela's Eggplant Parmesan

1 medium eggplant, peeled and sliced ½ to ¾ inch thick
Salt
Olive oil, divided
1 medium onion, sliced
4 medium tomatoes, peeled and cut into 6–8 wedges
Parmesan cheese, grated

Lay the eggplant on paper towels that have been generously salted. After salting the top(s) of the eggplant, cover with another layer of paper towels. Top with a heavy object such as a cutting board to help the towels absorb the moisture released from the eggplant. Let sit about 30 minutes.

Meanwhile, sauté the onion in 1 tablespoon olive oil for several minutes in a skillet or small saucepan that has a lid. Add the tomatoes and cover and cook until the tomatoes are tender, about 5 minutes. At this point you may remove the lid and cook further to reduce some of the liquid in the pan if desired. Season to taste with salt.

Heat broiler in oven. Remove eggplant from paper towels, wiping away any moisture that might remain on the eggplant. Place on a sheet pan that can go under your broiler. Brush the tops of the eggplant slices with oil. Broil until lightly browned. Remove from broiler. Using a spatula, turn the eggplant and brush the unoiled side of the slices with oil. Return to broiler and lightly brown the second side of the eggplant. Remove from broiler. Top slices with the tomato and onion mixture. Add Parmesan cheese to top of each slice. Return to broiler or hot oven to just melt the Parmesan. Remove and serve immediately. Serves 4.

Ratatouille

With eggplant and tomatoes and peppers available at the same time, late summer is a perfect time to make ratatouille. Because of all the veggies that need to be chopped, it can be time consuming to make, so try watching the Disney movie Ratatouille *and enlist any inspired children (or adults) around to help afterward.*

2 tablespoons cooking oil of choice
4–6 large garlic cloves, roughly chopped
2 large onions, cut into eighths
1 red pepper, cored, seeded, cut into eighths
1 yellow pepper, cored, seeded, cut into eighths
8 tomatoes, skinned, cored, cut into eighths
2 bay leaves
1 medium-large eggplant, peeled, cut into 1-inch pieces
2 medium zucchini, cut into ½-inch rounds
¼ cup basil leaves, packed
¼ cup parsley, packed
Salt and pepper to taste

Heat oven to 400 degrees. Heat the oil in a large ovenproof casserole or Dutch oven over medium heat. Sauté garlic briefly, but before it browns, add the onions and continue to cook until soft and fragrant. Add peppers and sauté 5 minutes longer. Add tomatoes and bay leaves and bring to a boil. Add in remaining ingredients, stirring briefly. Place in oven and bake for 1½–2 hours. Stir occasionally. Adjust seasoning and serve. Serves 4–6.

Okra

Ah, the much-maligned okra. It pains me every time someone accuses it of being slimy. I ate it minimally battered
and fried growing up, so I never even encountered this
notion until I was an adult. One must regard every feature
of each vegetable as an opportunity rather than a black
eye. The mucilaginous (slime) factor of okra helps thicken
soups or gumbo. I usually grew the hybrid 'Cajun Jewel'
for quantities but found some of the heirloom varieties
such as 'Clemson Spineless' or the seven-foot-tall 'Louisi-
ana Green Velvet' useful and exciting, too. The fuzzy, green,
tubular pods are best picked young at three to five inches.
The easiest way I enjoy okra is to sauté a small onion, add a
tomato or two, several trimmed and sliced okra pods, and
salt for a simple soup. When I have a lot, this soup freezes
well for winter pleasure.

Mother's Okra

1 pound okra, trimmed and sliced ¼-inch thick
1 egg
Flour
Corn meal
Oil
Salt
Pepper

Put the okra in a mixing bowl. Crack the egg and drop onto
the okra. Stir to blend well. Add in just enough flour and/or
corn meal to soak up the moisture of the egg and create a
thin breading. (I usually use a 50–50 mix.) In a skillet, heat
the oil over medium heat. Add the okra and cook until well

browned on one side, then turn to brown the other side, about 15 minutes total. Season with salt and pepper to taste. Serves 4.

VARIATION: Omit egg and corn meal. Limit flour to about 1 tablespoon and add a pinch of cayenne. This makes a drier version of fried okra but is a nice change of pace.

Roasted Okra with Sherry Mayonnaise

½ pound okra, washed and dried
1 tablespoon extra-virgin olive oil or another oil
Kosher salt

Sherry Mayonnaise
½ cup mayonnaise, preferably homemade
1 tablespoon sherry vinegar
1 tablespoon minced parsley
1 clove garlic, minced
1 teaspoon fresh lemon juice
Salt and pepper to taste

Preheat oven to 400 degrees. Place okra in a large bowl and toss well with the oil. Place in a single layer on a baking sheet. Bake for 20 minutes, turning halfway through. Meanwhile, prepare sherry mayonnaise, mixing all ingredients well, and set aside. Once okra is done, sprinkle with salt and serve immediately with dip on the side. (For a speedier version, skip the mayonnaise and eat the roasted okra plain after tossing it with kosher salt.)

Peppers

Green bell peppers are actually unripened peppers that will eventually turn some other color. It can be hard to wait several weeks longer, but the sweet results are certainly worth it. 'Ace' was my reliable sweet, red bell pepper standby, but 'Carmen' curried my favor, too—an Italian bull's-horn type just as sweet but more productive.

If you ever end up with too many peppers, they are easily frozen raw in plastic bags after halving and removing the core and seeds. Or you can roast them. There are several ways to roast peppers. You want to blister the skins for easy removal. This works best with thick-walled peppers. Bake them at 450 degrees for 20 minutes, turning them halfway through, or broil them, turning every 2–3 minutes until the skin blisters. This may also be accomplished by charring them over a gas stove flame or open grill. After charring, close the peppers in a paper bag for 15–20 minutes or longer. You may also just lay a towel over them. When cool enough to handle, peel the skin off the peppers, cut out the core, and remove the seeds. A third way I discovered is to roast them in a slow cooker. Rub the inside of your slow cooker with oil. Add 5–7 peppers, cut in half and seeded. Cook on high about 3 hours. Allow to cool. Peel. At this point, freeze them or use them.

Walter's Roasted Red Pepper Soup

*Walter Jahncke, co-owner of several restaurants, worked for
a time at the farm between jobs. I had eaten delicious pepper
soup at his restaurant Chat Noir in Des Moines, so I asked him
for a recipe. He recommended using your favorite tomato soup
recipe and substituting roasted peppers for some or all of the
tomatoes. He shared this one and said, "If you like this,
it's from me; if you don't, it came from a friend."*

1 red onion, diced
1 tablespoon olive oil
1 cup red wine (or vegetable stock or water)
2 pounds red peppers, roasted, peeled, coarsely cut
1 pound red tomatoes, peeled, coarsely cut
2 12-ounce cans tomato juice
1 bulb garlic, minced
Salt and white pepper to taste
Fresh basil leaves to taste (about 1 cup, loosely measured)
1 tablespoon balsamic vinegar
Water as needed

Sauté the onion in olive oil until translucent. Add red wine
and simmer for one minute. Add remaining ingredients
except basil and vinegar. Simmer about 20–30 minutes,
adding the basil the last 10 minutes. Remove from heat and
add vinegar. Purée if desired (being careful of hot liquid).
Add water to desired thickness. Serves 4.

Tomatoes

Open a Seed Savers Exchange seed catalog or other heirloom seed source and you will be amazed by all the choices
in tomatoes. Here you will find treasures that never show

up in a grocery store: 'Speckled Roman', 'Arkansas Traveler', 'Garden Peach', 'Green Zebra', 'Paul Robeson'. Is it any wonder that seed ordering during January can brighten even the dreariest winter day? The only thing better is to eat the first tomato of the season. This vegetable doesn't need much help for recipes, but I include a few just in case. Make sure to try the Cucumber, Onion, and Tomato Salad, page 167, and Onion Tart, page 187.

Scott's CSA Box Spaghetti Sauce
(or, A Lazy Man's Way of Storing Angela's Veggies for Winter)

2 pounds ground meat (beef, turkey, pork, sausage, whatever is
    hidden in your freezer), browned
2 cans tomato sauce
2 cans tomato paste
2 tomato paste cans of water (wine can be substituted for the water)
2 onions
Garlic
Italian spices
CSA box vegetables
Tabasco sauce, to taste
Sugar or artificial sweetener packet or two (if using sugar, add
    before last hour of cooking)

Put browned meat into Crock-Pot. Add remaining ingredients. Use CSA box vegetables such as onion, garlic, zucchini, squash, okra, peppers (hot or sweet), tomatoes, basil, celery, etc. Cook on low for 8–10 hours or on high for 5–6 hours. Eat what you want now and freeze the rest for good memories of Angela's vegetables. Serves 6–8. (From customer and friend Scott Shafer.)

THE SEPTEMBER CSA BOX

Leeks

Radish (Daikon)

Soybeans (Edamame)

Sweet Potatoes

Winter Squash

Leeks

On our visit to France's Brittany region, we traveled by car and could observe many fields of leeks, carrots, and other vegetables grown on a commercial scale—crops you wouldn't see in the fields of Iowa. Each home we passed also had leeks in their backyard gardens. French culture seems to appreciate leeks more than ours, I think. Leeks can, with proper mulching, survive Upper Midwest winters. (My preferred variety for that is 'Blue Solaise'.) I usually eat all mine before we get to that point.

Leek Potato Soup

2 tablespoons ghee or olive oil
1 large or 2 medium leeks, cleaned, trimmed, and thinly sliced,
    discarding dark green parts
2 stalks celery, chopped
1 large carrot, diced
2 large potatoes, preferably 'Yukon Gold' or similar, halved and
    thinly sliced
Chicken or vegetable broth
Salt and pepper
Optional herbs: thyme, bay leaf added during cooking time
¼–½ cup cream added at end of cooking time (optional)

Melt ghee in a large pot over medium heat. Add leeks and reduce heat, cooking slowly and stirring often so that they do not brown. Add celery and carrots about 5 minutes into this process. Cook 5 minutes longer. Add potatoes, broth, and herbs if using. Bring to a simmer and cook until potatoes are very soft. Remove bay leaf. Use a masher on the potatoes until a chunky mixture is obtained; if you prefer a smooth soup, you may use a hand blender. Add cream if desired. Season to taste. Serves 2–4.

Radish (Daikon)

A few of the vegetables I grew at Turtle Farm I had never grown, eaten, or cooked with before. Daikon radish is one of them. Like most radishes it is quite easy to grow in the fall with good results—so good in fact that they can almost outgrow the size of your forearm. It is often grated in salads or pickled. Daikon's inherent heat or spice was one reason I avoided it, but my fear was greater than the reality. Cooking it in a stew or other dishes, even roasting, tames the tang. For daikon radish ideas, I turned to customer and former chef Joel Severinghaus and his wife, Bev Westra, who serve wonderful Asian foods that we have personally enjoyed in the past. They report that "he makes miso soup using purchased miso, daikon, green onions, tofu cubes, mushrooms, Napa cabbage, or any combination of the above."

Soybeans (Edamame)

See Finger Lickin' Edamame with Garlic Sauce, page 185.

Sweet Potatoes

I primarily grew 'Beauregard' sweet potatoes at the farm because they were the easiest slips to obtain in quantity to plant. Other times it was also fun to try the many varieties that I could get from Sand Hill Preserve in Calamus, Iowa.

They have orange, yellow, white, and purple potatoes that vary in texture from moist to dry.

Be warned: mice love sweet potatoes. On the farm, the tubers were such a good food source that they often built their nests beneath the black weed fabric that we put on the potatoes to warm the soil and roots. It was heartbreaking at harvest to dig up or uncover the nests. Much squeaking and erratic darting would ensue. The mothers would run away, but if we stepped back from the scene for a few minutes, they would return and carry off their babies to a safe place.

If you grow your own sweet potatoes, be sure to cure them after harvest to ensure better texture and storage. I would put them in an unheated greenhouse in late summer that had temperatures in the 80s and 90s for at least several weeks. And don't wash them before they are cured, as washing can encourage spoilage. Even better, wait to wash them until you are ready to use them.

Sweet potato is another vegetable that can take a long time to cook whole. In the following recipes, they are diced, which can speed cooking. Grating, as mentioned with beets, can speed the process up even more. I have been known to grate a sweet potato to sauté quickly for breakfast. You could season with bacon, onion, mushrooms, rosemary, or orange.

Sweet Potato and Mushroom Pie

2 medium sweet potatoes, peeled and cut into ½-inch dice
1 medium onion, chopped
2 tablespoons oil
1 cup grated Gruyère cheese, divided
2 large eggs

½ teaspoon salt
¼ teaspoon pepper
3 slices bacon (substitute turkey bacon if desired)
8 ounces mushrooms, shitake or baby bella, cleaned and sliced
¼ cup white wine

Heat oven to 375 degrees. Place sweet potatoes and onion in a large bowl. Add the oil and toss. Place vegetables on a large baking sheet and put in oven to bake about 30 minutes or until tender. When done, return the mixture to the large bowl and coarsely mash with a potato masher. Add half the cheese and the eggs, salt, and pepper. Stir sweet potato mixture well and spoon this onto a nonstick cookie sheet, spreading evenly into a 10-inch circle or square. Bake for 10 minutes.

In a clean large skillet, cook bacon until just crisp. Drain on paper towel. When cool, break into small pieces. Reserve 2 tablespoons of bacon grease in skillet and sauté the mushrooms until lightly browned. Add the white wine and continue to cook until liquid is mostly evaporated. Set skillet off of heat.

When done, remove pie from oven. Spread the mushrooms, bacon, and remaining half cup cheese evenly over the sweet potatoes. Return to oven until the cheese melts, about 2 minutes. Serve immediately. Serves 2–4.

VARIATION: Use winter squash in place of sweet potato. (Adapted from allrecipes.com.)

Roasted Sweet Potato Salad

2 medium or 1 large sweet potato, peeled and cut into 1-inch cubes
1–2 tablespoons olive oil
½ teaspoon kosher salt
2 celery stalks, coarsely chopped
½ red pepper, thinly sliced
½ cup fruit such as pineapple chunks, peach slices, or dried currants

¼ cup walnuts, toasted
1 shallot or small onion, sliced into half-moons
1 tablespoon Dijon mustard
2 tablespoons mayonnaise
Salt and pepper

Preheat oven to 400 degrees. Toss the sweet potatoes with the olive oil and place on a baking sheet in a single layer. Bake potatoes 20 minutes or until tender, turning halfway through the cooking time. Remove and sprinkle with salt. Allow to cool slightly.

Meanwhile, mix together the remaining vegetables, fruit, and nuts in a large bowl. Add sweet potatoes. Mix mustard and mayonnaise and toss with salad. Adjust seasonings. Serves 4. (Adapted from *The Oprah Magazine Cookbook*, by Editors of *O Magazine*, 2008.)

Sweet Potato with Orange

2 medium sweet potatoes, peeled and cut into ¾-inch cubes
1–2 tablespoons olive oil
1 orange, zested (reserved), then peeled and sections separated
Salt to taste

Preheat oven to 375 degrees. Place the cubed sweet potatoes in a large bowl. Drizzle the olive oil over them and toss to coat. Place on baking sheet and bake for 20–30 minutes or until soft, turning midway through cooking time.

Meanwhile, place the orange in a food processor until well broken down. Place the cooked sweet potatoes into the food processor bowl with the orange. Pulse several times until just mixed. Add in orange zest and salt. Pulse again until desired consistency. Serve immediately while warm. Serves 2–4.

Winter Squash (including pumpkin)

Doing research with Dr. Mark Gleason from Iowa State University was helpful in figuring out ways to improve the survival of our winter squash crop. In the early years, in my haste to plant certain crops, thinking earlier was always better, the emerging squash would many times be eaten to the ground by voracious cucumber beetles before the plants could even form their true leaves. The beetles were hungry and would eat whatever was available because their usual food sources had not yet appeared. Planting later resulted in more successful crops.

Angela's Winter Squash Coconut Bisque

2 tablespoons ghee or coconut oil
1 cup chopped onion
3 garlic cloves, minced
1½-inch piece of ginger root, minced or grated
¼–½ teaspoon dried crushed red pepper
3 cups winter squash such as butternut or pumpkin, cooked
    and puréed
2 cups chicken or vegetable broth
½ cup raw cashews, soaked 4-6 hours in water to cover
1½ cup canned unsweetened coconut milk
Salt and pepper
Cilantro for garnish (optional)

Plan ahead to soak the cashews and bake the winter squash. Melt ghee or oil in large soup pot over medium heat. Add onion and sauté until translucent, about 10 minutes. Add garlic, ginger root, and crushed red pepper and briefly sauté. Then add pumpkin and broth. Bring to a boil. Reduce heat. Cover and simmer until flavors blend, about 30 minutes. In a food processor with blade, add drained cashews and process until smooth. Add a small amount of water to bring to a creamy texture. Being careful of hot liquid, purée several ladles of soup in food processor with the cashews until smooth. Return soup with cashews to pot and add coconut milk. Stir well and bring soup to a simmer. Season to taste with salt and pepper. Garnish with cilantro if desired. (A hand blender may be used to create a smoother texture if preferred.) Serves 4–6.

Pumpkin Apple Almond Muffins

1¼ cup almond meal
1 teaspoon cinnamon
¼ teaspoon nutmeg
¼ teaspoon ground ginger or thumb-sized piece of gingerroot, grated
¼ teaspoon allspice
½ teaspoon salt
2 teaspoons baking powder
½ cup chopped apples or applesauce
¾ cup pumpkin purée
2 eggs
2 tablespoons maple syrup or 1 tablespoon honey
1 teaspoon vanilla
¼–½ cup chocolate chips (optional)

Preheat oven to 350 degrees. Use a nonstick muffin pan or paper liners or grease well with butter or ghee. Mix dry ingredients and wet ingredients separately, then combine and stir just until moistened. Fold in desired amount of chocolate chips until barely mixed. Scoop approximately ½ cup batter into muffin cups or until three-fourths full. Bake at 350 degrees for 25 minutes until done when a toothpick inserted comes out clean. Allow to cool for 5 minutes. →

Remove from muffin tin to finish cooling on a wire rack. Makes 6–8 depending on size of muffin. (Adapted from wellplated.com.)

Mom's Pumpkin Pie

If you haven't tried using mace and allspice instead of cloves in your pumpkin pie, you might be pleasantly surprised by the difference. I find cloves to be too strong for my tastes. This is the pie I grew up on.

1½ cup cooked pumpkin, puréed or from a can
1 cup milk or light cream
½ cup sugar
1 teaspoon cinnamon
½ teaspoon salt
½ teaspoon allspice
¼ teaspoon mace
2 eggs
1 teaspoon vanilla
1 9-inch pie shell, prepared
1 tablespoon butter, melted (optional)

Preheat oven to 425 degrees. Mix all ingredients (except pie shell and butter) in a large bowl. Put into prepared pie shell. Add butter on top. Place in oven and bake 15 minutes. Reduce heat to 350 degrees and bake an additional 35–40 minutes until a knife inserted halfway between the center and edge of the crust comes out clean.

TIP: You can skip the crust and make this as a custard. Without the crust, bake at 350 degrees about 35–40 minutes, testing for doneness as mentioned above.

Raw Butternut Squash Salad with Walnuts and Cranberries

1 small butternut squash, peeled and grated, about 3 cups
⅓ cup dried cranberries
3 green onions or 1 shallot, sliced thinly
2 tablespoons parsley, chopped
⅓ cup walnuts

Dressing

1 tablespoon lime juice
1 tablespoon lemon juice
2 tablespoons olive oil
Salt and pepper to taste

Toast walnuts in a 350-degree oven for 4–5 minutes, watching closely that they do not burn. Set aside to cool slightly. Mix remaining salad ingredients together in a large bowl. Add cooled walnuts to salad bowl. Combine dressing ingredients in a small bowl and whisk together. Add to salad and toss well. Add salt and pepper to taste. Serves 2–4.

Spaghetti Squash with Pesto

1 small spaghetti squash
2 cups cooked chicken, cubed or shredded (optional for vegan)
2 tablespoons basil pesto (see Pesto, page 191)
½ cup chicken or vegetable broth
2 tablespoons pine nuts, slightly toasted

Preheat oven to 375 degrees. Split the spaghetti squash in half and place in baking pan to cook until tender, about 45 minutes. When done, set aside to cool. When cool enough to handle or using hot pads, shred the squash fibers into "spaghetti" with a fork. Place in a large skillet along with the remaining ingredients, mixing well, and heat until dish is hot. Serves 2–4.

THE OCTOBER CSA BOX

Brussels Sprouts

Shallots

Brussels Sprouts

If you want to impress someone with this vegetable, give them the whole "spine" or stalk of Brussels sprouts. The first year I grew them, the 'Diablo' variety grew waist high. A tip for growers is to cut off the upper stem with leaves the first of September to end the creation of additional sprouts and to stimulate the existing ones to expand. And don't forget to eat those Brussels sprout leaves as a green.

Baby Brussels Sprouts with Buttered Pecans

¼ cup pecan halves
1 tablespoon butter
¼ teaspoon salt
1 pound Brussels sprouts, trimmed and halved, small size preferred
1 tablespoon ghee
1 large garlic clove, minced
Fresh lemon juice
Salt and pepper to taste

Preheat oven to 400 degrees. Spread pecans on a baking sheet and bake in oven until just fragrant, about 2–3 minutes. Watch carefully that they do not burn. Remove pecans to a small bowl, add butter and salt, and toss until butter is melted and nuts are coated.

Meanwhile, cook Brussels sprouts in large pan of boiling salted water until just tender, about 5–7 minutes depending on size. Transfer to a large bowl of ice water to stop cooking. Drain in a colander. Pat dry.

Melt ghee in a large skillet over medium heat. Add Brussels sprouts, sautéing and stirring occasionally until starting to brown, about 5–7 minutes. Add garlic for the last several minutes of cooking. Remove from heat, add a squeeze of lemon juice, pepper, and salt to taste. Stir in pecans and serve. Serves 4. (Adapted from Epicurious.com.)

Fall Shredded Brussels Sprouts Salad

This salad won best recipe at our 2016 Iowa Food Co-op potluck dinner. It was brought by friend and former employee Linda Hanson.

12 ounces Brussels sprouts, tough outer leaves removed
¼ cup dried cranberries
¼ cup chopped, roasted pecans
¼ cup Gorgonzola cheese crumbles
1 pear, chopped
2 tablespoons extra-virgin olive oil
2 jumbo shallots, thinly sliced

Maple-Balsamic Vinaigrette

2 tablespoons extra-virgin olive oil
2 tablespoons balsamic vinegar
1 tablespoon maple syrup (not pancake syrup)
1 teaspoon Dijon mustard
Salt and pepper

Using a sharp knife, thinly shred Brussels sprouts while holding onto the core end, then discard remaining core. Add shredded sprouts to a large bowl with dried cranberries, pecans, cheese, and pear. Set aside.

Heat oil in a skillet over medium-high heat. Add one shallot and fry until light golden brown, 1–2 minutes. Scoop onto a paper towel–lined plate to drain. Repeat with remaining shallot. Sprinkle with salt then let cool slightly. Mix together ingredients for vinaigrette in a jar, then shake to combine. Pour over the salad and toss to coat. Add fried shallots, toss to combine, and serve. Serves 4. (From iowa girleats.com.)

Shallots

I discovered these alliums store longer than their onion cousins. So in late winter when all my onions have been used up or sprouted, I make this yummy winter salad composed with shallots.

Winter Sprout Salad with Orange and Avocado

1 shallot, thinly sliced
2 cup sprouts (use a variety such as broccoli, radish, sunflower, or pea)
Olive oil
Lime juice
Salt and pepper to taste
½ to 1 avocado, thinly sliced
Orange, peeled, divided in half, and sliced into half circles

Place the shallots and sprouts in a small bowl. Drizzle with a little olive oil and a squeeze of lime juice. Add desired salt and pepper. Toss gently until well coated. Arrange the mixture onto two small salad plates. Lay the avocado and orange slices in an alternating circular pattern on top of the sprouts. Drizzle a little more lime juice over the avocado. Serves 2.

"Thank you again, everyone, for making
seventeen great years possible for Turtle Farm.
I never imagined it would be such a delightful
adventure. I never imagined I would meet
so many interesting people. . . ."

—*TURTLE TIMES,* OCTOBER 30, 2012

HOW TO GET THE MOST
OUT OF YOUR CSA

A Tip Sheet
for the
Agriculturally
Curious

Who should join a CSA?

IF YOU ARE THINKING OF JOINING this evolutionary eating, charitable eating, Zen eating, environmental eating, or whatever kind of eating motivates you in this direction, here are questions to ask yourself to see if a CSA will be a good fit for you. A CSA is not for everyone, and there are other ways to support local producers and eat healthy if you choose not to join one.

- Are you willing to eat a wide variety of fresh organic produce that is provided over the course of the growing season?
- Do you have time each week to pick up, clean, and prepare your food?
- Can you give up some of the convenience of grocery store shopping to support a local farmer and that farm connection?

- Will you be around most of the growing season to receive your produce?

- Can you afford to share the costs of supporting the farm, including the risks?

- Can you accept less than beautiful produce, and recognize and value priceless food rather than expecting cheap food?

- Are you a creative cook, able to pivot with what you get each week? Can you look at the box and see dinner—for example, ratatouille or a stir-fry?

- Do you have the food storage space needed for the box of veggies you will get?

- Are you willing to understand and accept the farm, weather, and pest interactions of food production?

- Do you want to be a part of a sustainable movement of revolutionary eating? Can you look beyond the romance or nostalgia of the CSA idea to the real practicalities of dealing with the produce week after week?

- How many vegetables do you normally eat at home and how often do you eat out? Would finding someone to share a box with work better for you as an introduction? Or can you ask friends who are in a CSA to let you take their box when they are on vacation to see what the process is like?

- Do you understand that you will still be visiting the grocery store or markets to fill in the gaps of what you need or want that doesn't come in the box that week?

- Can you accept an occasional bug or some dirt on your produce?

Which CSA should you join?

Every CSA is different. Assuming there is more than one that is a possibility for you to join, you might consider these tips or questions when selecting one.

- Word of mouth from friends and acquaintances who are in a CSA is a good place to start.
- Do your values fit the mission of your CSA choice?
- What do they grow and how long is their season?
- Is there flexibility to mix and match veggies of your choice?
- Does their delivery time and location of drop-offs work for you?
- Can you conveniently visit the farm, and are there opportunities to meet with the farmer face to face before joining, as well as after becoming a member?
- What is the cost and is there any choice in how to pay for the share?
- Visit www.localharvest.com to find CSAs in your area and brief descriptions of their operations as well as contact information. There are many kinds of CSAs.

Who should start a CSA?

- If you are not already a farmer, you might consider trying an internship or working on a variety of farms.
- Do you have crop management, production, and equipment skills?
- Do you have people skills?
- Do you have technology, communication, and teaching skills?
- Do you have access to land, water, and markets?
- Are you familiar with food, tastes, varieties, and uses of the crops to understand what cooks may be looking for?

Book Resources for CSA Members

Eating on the Wild Side: The Missing Link to Optimum Health, by Jo Robinson (Little, Brown and Company, 2014).

Farmer John's Cookbook: The Real Dirt on Vegetables, by Farmer John Peterson and Angelic Organics (Gibbs Smith, 2006).

From Asparagus to Zucchini: A Guide to Cooking Farm-Fresh Seasonal Produce, by the Madison Area Community Supported Agriculture Coalition, 1st, 2nd, and 3rd editions (MACSAC, 1996, 2003, 2004).

Local Flavors: Cooking and Eating from America's Farmers' Markets, by Deborah Madison (Broadway Books, 2008).

The New Vegetarian Cooking for Everyone, by Deborah Madison (Ten Speed Press, 2014).

Nourishing Traditions, by Sally Fallon (NewTrends Publishing, 2001).

Vegetarian Cooking for Everyone, by Deborah Madison (Broadway Books, 1997).

The Whole Life Nutrition Cookbook: Whole Foods Recipes for Personal and Planetary Health, by Alissa Segersten and Tom Malterre (Whole Life Press, 2007).

Book Resources for CSA Farmers

Four Season Harvest: How to Harvest Fresh, Organic Vegetables from Your Home Garden All Year Long, by Eliot Coleman (Chelsea Green Publishing, 1999).

How to Grow More Vegetables Than You Ever Thought Possible on Less Land Than You Can Imagine, by John Jeavons (Ten Speed Press, 2017).

The New Organic Grower: A Master's Manual of Tools and Techniques for the Home and Market Gardener, by Eliot Coleman, 2nd edition (Chelsea Green Publishing, 1995).

Sharing the Harvest: A Citizen's Guide to Community Supported Agriculture, by Elizabeth Henderson, with Robyn Van En (Chelsea Green Publishing, 2007).

Sustainable Vegetable Production from Start-Up to Market, by Vernon Grubinger (Natural Resource, Agriculture, and Engineering Service, 1999).

ACKNOWLEDGMENTS

I THANK MY PARENTS for planting the seeds of my passion by introducing me to my first gardens and teaching me how to bring the rewards to the table.

Strong roots evolved from networking with my many farming colleagues through Iowa Network for Community Agriculture, Practical Farmers of Iowa, Iowa State University, and beyond. Your inspiration and support were ever present.

I am grateful to all my CSA customers who put their trust in me and fertilized the seeds I cast upon the soil to sprout and grow.

A nod goes to Catherine Cocks for voicing a different vision to pursue in my writing. Many thanks to Mary Swander, who rescued my idea for this book by weeding out extraneous materials and pointing it in the right direction. Thank you, Kelsey Leopard, for the second cultivation. John Obrycki graciously contributed entomological advice.

Thank you to editor Kristian Tvedten and others at the University of Minnesota Press for guiding me and pruning the manuscript into a presentable final product.

Like the sun that shines, I thank John for his loving support in so many ways on this growing journey. I am also grateful to Gaia for her nurturance and abundant harvests.

For seventeen years **ANGELA TEDESCO** was owner and operator of Turtle Farm, twenty acres near Granger, Iowa, that was one of the state's first certified organic CSA farms. She is a founding member of the Iowa Network for Community Agriculture, has served on the board of Practical Farmers of Iowa, and is a contributor to *The Future of Family Farms: Practical Farmers' Legacy Letter Project,* edited by Teresa Opheim. Now retired, she lives in Johnston, Iowa.